W9-BYY-262

How to
Fix
Stuff

How to Fix Stuff

Tom Scalisi

Tanya Watson

Additional text by

Sam Martin

THUNDER BAY
P·R·E·S·S

San Diego, California

Contents

1: HOME REPAIRS

2: DECORATING & UPCYCLING

3: DOMESTIC HACKS

5: BACKYARD & SHED HACKS

4: EXTERIOR FIXES

How to Use This Book

You are either already a handy person or you aspire to be. The 59 projects in this book will not only save you money by not having to call a professional, but they'll make you a proud homeowner/renter as well. Through simple step-by-step instructions and diagrams, you don't need to have any previous DIY experience to get these projects done.

First we will take you through the basics: figuring out which tools you need and different ways you can learn to use them (and become more handy in the process!) and the all-important safety measures that come with doing any kind of DIY.

Then we roll up our sleeves and get to work! The projects are organized into five chapters: Home Repairs, Decorating & Upcycling, Domestic Hacks, Exterior Fixes, and Backyard & Shed Hacks. Throughout you'll find Handy Hints, as well as aspirational photographs to keep you motivated. Our goal is to cover every aspect of your home and domestic life: from fixing a clogged sink to installing wainscotting, from reattaching a bag strap to changing a skateboard wheel, from repairing a roof shingle to hanging outdoor lighting.

Finally, we'll give you some advice about where to buy your tools and what to look for when shopping, as well as a very handy index to all the projects included in the book.

How to Fix Stuff is the essential handbook for tackling common problems and maintaining the perfect home. So grab your hammer, screwdriver—and safety glasses—and start fixing!

What Tools Do I Need?

YOU DON'T NEED TO BUY a lot of fancy equipment or brand-new top-of-the-line tools if you're using them occasionally for small jobs. But if your first tools are the start of a collection you intend to expand over the years, it's worth spending extra for quality. Sometimes it can make sense to rent rather than to buy. This is especially true when you need an expensive or more specialized piece of equipment you may use just once. Answer the following questions and you'll have a strategy to guide your purchases:

- What tasks do you want to perform?
- How much use do you expect to get from your tools?
- How involved are the projects you want to take on?
- How much do you want to spend?
- How much space do you have?

There are several ways of learning how to use tools. Continuing education classes are a good way to learn the basics. You may need to provide your own hand tools and materials, but the school will provide access to try larger or more expensive tools. This can be a helpful way to use tools without making a large investment in equipment.

Persuade a knowledgable and experienced friend to work with you on a project. Just holding the flashlight or fetching the tools is a chance to watch how it's done, ask questions, and learn. You can also consider working a part-time or summer job, if you're young or retired, to help out a contractor or work in a maintenance department. At best, you'll pick up some new skills and earn some pocket money. At worst, it will convince you to stay in college or remind you why you retired.

For more information on where to buy tools, see page 186.

Safety First

IT'S EASIER TO CUT THINGS OFF than stick them back on. This is as true for fingers and toes as it is for wood and metal.

Working with tools involves a degree of risk. You can reduce the risk by using common sense and paying attention to what you are doing. When working, consider several factors: your ability, the worked materials, your equipment, and your surroundings. Each of these things should be under your control. When you are drowsy, distracted, or not 100 percent focused, mistakes happen. At best you will have ruined your project by rushing it, or at worst, you will injure yourself.

First, make sure other people, especially children, are safely out of harm's way before you start working. Prepare by looking over a project and assembling your tools and materials before you dive in. Dress appropriately: if you are using anything with motors or moving parts, don't wear loose or flowing clothes or jewelry. If you have long hair, tie it back. You don't want to get anything caught or tangled in a machine. Wear decent shoes to avoid slipping and protect your feet from falling or sharp objects. Use any safety gear appropriate to the tool in use. Personal protection gear needs to fit properly. If a device is uncomfortable, distracting, or otherwise hindering, seek out an alternative that's better for you.

Know how your tool works and how it should be operated. Don't disable any safety guards or devices. Don't force a tool to do a job for which it is not intended. If you are learning to use a tool, practice on some scrap until you feel comfortable and familiar with how it behaves. Mistakes happen and sometimes a tool behaves unexpectedly. Learn from these mistakes and figure out why they occurred. If you are unsure, ask someone: something may be wrong with the tool or your technique.

Maintain your tools by keeping them clean. Keep cutters and blades sharp. A sharp tool is safer than a dull one because the blade moves smoothly through the work. Forcing a dull blade through the work piece can lead to accidents.

Cluttered work areas are hazardous, and you can also waste a lot of time looking for tools. Hastily run extension cords are particularly dangerous. Be aware of your actions and movements and think out the technique before you start a particular task. Where are you and your hands positioned in relation to the tool? Will these positions change as the work progresses? Where will the tool go if it should slip? Where will your hands go if they too should slip? Think ahead and always anticipate what could go wrong and adjust your setup to avoid any nasty consequences.

Finally, know the limits of your skills and knowledge, and don't bite off more than you can chew. If possible, plan your projects to build on the experience of your previous ones. By learning to manage the risks involved with working with tools, your projects will be safer, more enjoyable, and ultimately more successful and satisfying.

HAZARDS TO REMEMBER

Pesticide treatment applied to pressure-treated lumber contains arsenic and should never be used indoors.

Paints, finishes, and solvents containing dangerous fumes should be worked only in well-ventilated areas and be stored away from potential sparks, flames, or other heat sources.

Long-term exposure to sawdust has been shown to cause respiratory problems. Wear a dust mask or respirator to protect your lungs when sanding, cutting, or working with drywall and concrete.

Dispose of waste and debris in a safe and environmentally sound manner. Read the product's label or ask the retailer if there are any special precautions to take for disposal.

Spread out paint or solvent-soaked rags to dry in a well-ventilated area prior to disposal. Don't toss wadded-up rags into the trash as the heat generated by the evaporation of any solvent can cause combustion.

Do not burn pressure-treated lumber and aerosol cans.

1

Home Repairs

How to Patch a Hole in a Wooden Floor

HARDWOOD FLOORS LOOK AMAZING. Whether they be hardwood or an antique wide-plank variety, their warmth and coziness are one of a kind. But even though wooden floorboards are a fairly durable choice, the words "durable" and "indestructible" have different meanings. Holes in a wooden floor can happen for a host of reasons. Perhaps you're renovating a room and moving heating pipes. Or maybe someone was dragging something heavy across the surface and dug into the wood, causing deep gouges. These things happen. Luckily, patching a hole in a wooden floor isn't as hard as it seems. When patching a hole in a wooden floor, you aren't filling the hole. You're actually removing an entire plank and replacing it with a new one. If the hole lands on a seam between two or three boards, they'll all need replacing.

YOU WILL NEED

Varying lengths of matching tongue-and-groove wood in the same width and thickness

Masking tape

Circular saw

Table saw

Pry bar

Tape measure

Miter saw

Hammer

2½-inch (6cm) lost-head nails

Nail set

HOW TO

1 Use masking tape to protect the flooring on either side of the board in question. This will prevent unnecessary scratches and scuffs.

2 Adjust the blade depth on the circular saw to just over ¾ inch (2cm), which is the typical thickness for hardwood flooring. With the blade parallel to the long sides of the board, carefully perform a "plunge cut" in the middle (see Fig. A). Continue this cut from one end of the board to the other, being careful not to overrun the ends.

3 Use a pry bar placed into the cut to separate the floorboard. It will likely crack and come out in two long pieces. This step will expose the subfloor underneath.

4 You need to get creative with the tongues and grooves on the replacement piece. Start by measuring the empty space left by the damaged board.

5 Hook the tape measure to the grooved end of the new piece of hardwood, mark it to length, and cut it on a miter saw. For the board to drop into place, use a table saw to remove only the bottom lip on the grooved side and end of the board. Typically, this involves raising the blade to slightly more than ¼ inch (0.6cm) and setting the fence approximately ½–¾ inch (1.2–2cm) from the blade.

continues

Fig. A

continued

6 Placing the new piece's tongue into the existing groove first, lay the board into the gap (see Fig. B).

7 Blunt the tips of several 2½-inch (6cm) lost-head nails with a hammer to prevent them from splitting the wood. Drive a pair of these nails through the new board and into the subfloor every 6–8 inches (15–20cm) (see Fig. C). Use a nail set to drive the head below.

8 Sand the floor and stain the new pieces to match.

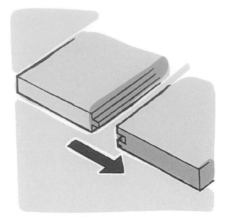

Fig. B

Fig. C

HANDY HINTS

Be careful not to damage any good existing floorboards. Tape will prevent scuffs, but it won't stop a saw blade.

Don't drive any nails within 1 inch (2.5cm) of the groove side of the board or they may split the groove. Also, hold the final sets of nails back about 1½ inches (4cm) from either end of the board to prevent splitting.

How to Repair a Hole in Drywall

MOST HOLES IN DRYWALL occur by flinging open a door, causing the doorknob to leave a gash. Luckily, holes are fairly easy to repair. Just be sure you know where your electrical wires are before cutting into drywall. They are usually attached to wall studs, so locate your wall studs before starting to repair any drywall.

YOU WILL NEED

Drywall saw

Stanley knife

Scraps of drywall

Drill

Joint compound

Putty knife

Joint tape

Fine-grit sandpaper

HOW TO

1 If the hole is roundish in shape, use a drywall saw and turn the round hole into a square one. Make sure there is no loose plaster or paper around the perimeter of the hole. If there is, break or cut it off, using a Stanley knife.

2 Cut a piece of drywall to the same size as the hole plus about 2 inches (5cm) all around. This is the backer board. Drill a finger-size hole in the middle of the backer board.

3 Run a bead of joint compound on the backer board, around the outer edges of its face so that it will stick to the wall behind the hole (see Fig. A). Put the backer board inside the hole and, using your finger and the finger hole, hold it in place for several minutes, until the compound takes hold.

4   Now cut a piece of plasterboard to the same size as the hole. This is the patch. Smear joint compound on the back of the patch. Fit the patch into the hole with its back resting against the backer board and hold it there briefly until the compound dries.

5   Spread a light layer of joint compound along the edges of the patch using a putty knife, then push joint tape into the hole filler (see Fig. B). Cover the tape with another layer of joint compound and smooth more compound over the entire patch, making sure you blend the edges into the surrounding drywall. Let it dry.

6   After the hole filler has dried, sand it smooth all over, using the fine-grit sandpaper. Paint the wall to hide the patch altogether.

Fig. A

Fig. B

How to Fix a Dripping Faucet

FIXING A DRIPPING FAUCET is quite easy to do and won't take too much of your time. The most common kinds of faucets are two-handled hot and cold ones and single-handled cartridge faucets. Usually, the cause of a dripping two-handled faucet is a worn-out washer, which you can access through either handle. For a single-handled faucet, you'll need to replace the cartridge or stem, so be sure you know which one you'll need, as there are many different types. The best way to do this is to take the old one to the store with you.

YOU WILL NEED

Screwdriver
(flat-head or Phillips,
depending on the
faucet)

Adjustable wrench

Cloth

Needle-nose pliers

New washer
(for a two-handle
faucet)

New cartridge
(for a single-handled
faucet)

HOW TO

1 Turn off the main water valve. Find this by
looking under your sink for pipes that run
up. Somewhere along these pipes will be
handles—twist these clockwise to shut them
off. Turn the faucets on so any remaining
water empties into the sink.

2 Determine if it's the hot or cold water that's
dripping. If the faucet has a cap, remove it
with a flat-head screwdriver (see Fig. A).

continues

Fig. A

> ### HANDY HINT
> Plug the drain before you get started
> to make sure that you don't lose
> any screws or washers down the
> plughole.

Fig. B

Fig. C

3 Then unscrew the top of the handle with the appropriate screwdriver. If your faucet has a decorative "bonnet" under the handle, use an adjustable wrench to remove it, covering the bonnet with a cloth to avoid scratching it.

4 What you see now is the packing nut. Use an adjustable wrench to unscrew the nut and pull out the entire stem assembly from the handle (see Figs. B and C).

5 At the base of the stem is the washer. Replace it (see Fig. D) and put the handle back together.

6 For a single-handled cartridge faucet, unscrew the handle and the bonnet and grab the cartridge or stem that regulates the flow of hot and cold water with a pair of needle-nose pliers. Pull it straight up and out.

Fig. D

7 Replace the cartridge, making sure it is aligned properly, and put the assembly back together. Turn the water back on and run the faucet(s) for a few minutes.

HANDY HINT

If your faucet is not dripping but is leaking at the handle, it is more than likely that the rubber O-ring at the top of the stem or around the cartridge is worn out. To get to it, take off the handle and bonnet. The O-ring will be just under the packing nut and is easy to replace. Simply cut the old O-rings off with a utility knife. Coat the replacement O-rings in plumber's grease, and install them according to the manufacturer's instructions.

How to Unblock a Sink

CLOGGED SINKS ARE AMONG the most common household problems, largely because food debris and soap residue are nightmares for smooth draining. Thankfully, clogged drains are also fairly easy to fix yourself. Here are four methods to try before calling the plumber.

The first method is the easiest. Simply bring half a gallon of water to a boil. Pour the boiling water down the clogged drain. If necessary, repeat. If the sink is still clogged—or if your drain is connected to a PVC pipe (boiling water could melt it or cause damage)—move on to the next method. Next, try unclogging it with a plunger. A flat-bottomed plunger works best for sinks. Run a little water into the sink (an inch or two). Plunge away, making sure you get a nice flat connection to the sink.

If that doesn't work, pour a liquid chemical-based cleaner into the drain, following manufacturer's instructions. If the sink is still blocked, use a plumber's snake to clean it. Push the snake gently into the drain. As it goes in, rotate it until it breaks through or dislodges the debris and then pull it out.

Another way to unblock a sink is to unscrew and clean out the trap. Place a pan under the trap and use an adjustable wrench to remove the clean-out plug. If there's no clean-out plug, remove the whole trap and clean out any debris.

HANDY HINT

If you don't have liquid cleaner on hand, you can use baking soda and white vinegar. Start by pouring boiling water down the drain, followed by ⅓ cup (65g) of baking soda with 1 cup (250ml) of white vinegar. Once you hear it fizzing, wait 10 minutes and then run hot water for a few minutes more.

How to Replace a Cracked Ceramic Tile

NOT ONLY DO CRACKED OR LOOSE bathroom tiles look unattractive, but the cracks will gather mold and mildew faster than you can clean them. Thankfully, it's quite easy to replace damaged tiles. Just be careful not to let any grout dry on the face of any tile. But if you do, you can remove dried grout with a little paint thinner.

YOU WILL NEED

Grout saw

Hammer

Chisel

Putty knife

Tile adhesive

Masking tape

Rubber gloves

Grout

HOW TO

1 Using a grout saw, scrape out the grout around the broken tile (see Fig. A).

2 Use a hammer and chisel to gently break out the tile and remove the pieces from the wall (see Fig. B). Also use the chisel or putty knife to remove any dried adhesive behind the tile so that the wall surface is totally flat.

3 Using a putty knife, smear a good amount of tile adhesive on the back of the new tile. Press it into place until it is flush with the surrounding wall. Tape the tile in place and allow the adhesive to dry, as per manufacturer directions. Remove the tape when dried.

4 Put on rubber gloves and, using the putty knife, press grout into the gaps around the new tile.

5 After 15 minutes, wipe off any excess grout with a wet rag. If there are gaps or holes in the grout, apply more, let it set for 15 minutes, and wipe the excess off again. Let the grout fully dry for a few days before getting the tiles wet.

Fig. A

Fig. B

HANDY HINT

If you don't have extra tiles, take your cracked tile to the store to find a match in both size and thickness. If you don't have the original grout, smear a bit of the grout you do have on a thick piece of paper and let it dry overnight. Then compare it to the grout around your tiles to make sure it matches.

How to Fix a Burst Pipe

PIPES BURST OR CRACK in cold weather when the water inside them expands as it freezes. Prevent burst pipes in the first place by installing a stop-and-waste valve on water lines, allowing you to drain water out of pipes before the temperature drops. You can also insulate outdoor or basement pipes with a foam-plastic pipe insulation.

YOU WILL NEED

Duct tape

Epoxy glue or paste

C-clamp

Hose clamp

Rubber pad

Screwdriver

HOW TO

1 If the crack looks small and the leak is gradual, it may be possible to wrap the pipe with duct tape without turning off the main water supply. Make sure you overlap each pass of tape as you cover the crack (see Fig. A).

2 A more permanent patch can be made with store-bought epoxy glue or paste, especially if the crack is near a pipe joint. Before applying any epoxy, the water must be turned off and the pipe must be thoroughly dry.

3 For a larger crack, turn the water off once you have located the leak, then place a rubber pad over the crack and around the pipe.

4 Put half the C clamp over the rubber, on top of the pipe. Fit the other half of the clamp in place so that it surrounds the rubber and the pipe, and screw the two halves together (see Fig. B). (If you don't have a pipe clamp, a hose clamp— or two or three—will also work.)

5 If you've turned the water off to patch the leak, turn it back on and observe the patched section of pipe to make sure it's not leaking anymore.

Fig. A

Fig. B

HANDY HINT

If there is any water damage, get to it quickly to prevent any kind of mold growth. Grab a mop, a bucket or two, and a shop vacuum, if necessary, to get rid of any sitting water first so that it doesn't soak through to another part of the house. Then scrub any moldy hard surfaces with a mild household bleach solution.

How to Draft-proof a Room

DOES ANYTHING TURN A COZY NIGHT on the couch into a chilling affair more than a drafty room? Air pouring in from the windows, the door, or the electric outlets can make a room downright uncomfortable. Those drafts also sap the bank account when the utility bill shows up. If only there were a way to draft-proof a room, restore its coziness, and keep the utility company at bay.

Good news: a way exists. Several, in fact. The most common areas where outside air can penetrate a home are the windows, exterior doors, and outlets or light switches. There are simple, cost-effective ways to take care of each.

Latex caulk

Caulking gun

Door draft
stopper

Doorjamb
insulation kit

Pencil

Hacksaw or scissors

Tape
measure

Hand saw

Hammer

Screwdriver

Power drill

Wall plate insulation
gaskets

HOW TO

1 Use the caulk and caulking gun to apply a
bead of caulk all around a drafty window.
Start on the inside of the window frame.
Caulk where the jamb meets the window
on the top, bottom, and sides. Next, apply
caulk where the window trim and jamb meet
(usually just the top and sides). Finally,
run a bead of caulk around the outside of
the window trim where it meets the wall.
Don't forget under the sill and the apron
underneath, too.

2 Hold the draft stopper at the inside bottom
of a drafty door, aligning one edge with the
edge of the door. Use the pencil to mark it
to the width of the door and cut it to length.
Use scissors for a foam or rubber stopper or
a hacksaw for a metal stopper. Foam draft
stoppers slide under the door while rubber
versions adhere with double-sided tape.
Draft stoppers with metal frames require
using a screwdriver or power drill and
screwing in place (see Fig. A).

Fig. A

continues

continued

3 Step outside and close the door behind you. Measure and cut the top piece of trim using a hacksaw or hand saw. Hold the cut piece in place so the foam weather stripping touches the door without completely crushing the foam (see Figs. B and C). Use the included nails to nail it in place. Continue with each side piece, being careful to cut the square end, not the curved end that fits snugly around the top piece.

Fig. B

4 Remove the drafty outlet cover or switch plate from the outlet face. Remove a drafty cover switch plate from the wall. Punch the required shape out of the insulation gasket (they're pre-scored). Place the gasket on the inside of the cover plate, line up the screws, and fasten the switch plate cover in place.

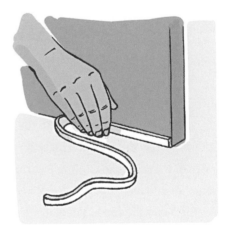

Fig. C

How to Replace a Windowpane

THE BIGGEST HURDLE when replacing a windowpane in an old wooden frame is that you have to fix it from the outside. If you can't because it's too far off the ground, you should remove the entire window sash from the frame and bring it inside. In most instances, you should be able to tackle the job without the help of a professional.

YOU WILL NEED

New pane of glass, measured to fit the window opening

Leather gloves

Putty knife

Chisel

Pliers

Fine-grit sandpaper

Oil-based primer paint

Paintbrush

Glazing putty

HOW TO

1 Put on leather gloves and remove any broken glass from the window sash. Scrape off any old glazing putty with a stiff putty knife or chisel and remove the glazing points that hold the glass with pliers (see Fig. A).

2 Sand the window sash smooth and paint on a coat of primer. After the primer has dried, take the putty knife and apply a thin layer of putty to the window sash to act as a bed for the new glass.

3 Put the new piece of glass in place and push it gently into the putty. To secure it in place, push in new glazing points with a chisel, 2 inches (5cm) from each corner and 6 inches (15cm) apart.

Fig. A

Fig. B

4 Scoop out some glazing putty with your hands and roll it into a thin rope. Press this around the perimeter of the glass with your fingers to cover the glazing sprigs and seal the glass to the sash (see Fig. B). Smooth out the glazing putty with a putty knife so that you end up with a neat, triangular bead of putty around the entire window.

5 After allowing the putty to dry for a week to 10 days, paint the glazing to match the color of the exterior sash.

HANDY HINT

When you paint the new glazing putty, overlap the paint onto the glass to create a watertight seal between the window and the putty. Then, when the paint dries, use a razor blade to scrape the glass clean of extra paint and putty.

How to Replace a Screen

JUST LIKE THE REST OF YOUR HOUSE EXTERIOR, window screens can start to look worn and shabby as they get older. Not only is it important to keep them clean with a bristle brush and some water, but when holes, tears, and general wear give your screens that run-down look, they should be replaced altogether.

YOU WILL NEED

Flat-head screwdriver

Fine mesh screen:
it should measure a little wider and 6 inches (15cm) longer than the screen opening

Spline roller

Utility knife

Staple gun

Pair of upholstery-stretcher pliers

Hammer

Panel pins, or tacks

HOW TO

1 If you are working with a metal frame, use the screwdriver to pry the screen spline from the frame. If you are working with a wooden frame, use the screwdriver to pry the molding off, and then to remove the staples. Remove the screen.

2 Lay the new screen in position, making sure it fits both sides and at the bottom. It should overlap the frame by 6 inches (15cm) at the top. Use a spline roller to press the spline back in place and trim any excess screen with a utility knife.

3 Staple the bottom edge to the wood frame. Using upholstery pliers, grab the middle of the screen at the top and use the frame as a fulcrum to pull the screen tight. Staple the top edge of the screen to the wood frame, starting in the middle (see Fig. A).

4 Work your way out to one corner, pulling the screen with the pliers and stapling every ½ inch (1.2cm) and then work your way to the opposite corner in the same manner.

5 Staple the screen to both sides of the wood frame.

6 Cut off the excess screen, and use a hammer and panel pins, or tacks, to fix the molding back in place (see Fig. B).

Fig. A

Fig. B

How to Rewire a Lamp

IF THE WIRING of your favorite lamp has been
damaged, or perhaps it's just very old and has become
unsafe, don't throw the lamp out! Give it new life by
rewiring it. Rewiring a lamp is an easy task and a
replacement plug and cord—even the socket—are easy
to find in hardware stores. Follow these steps to rewire
your favorite lamp. A word of caution: new lamp cords
have polarity, hot and neutral. You can sometimes
identify which is which by feeling the cord halves:
one side is smooth and one side has a ridge—the side
with the ridge is the neutral and the smooth side is
the hot. If the wire is color coded: hot is white, black
is neutral. Mixing up the wires can cause shocks, so
pay attention!

Utility knife

Electrical tape

Flat-head or Phillips
screwdriver

Wire strippers

New cord with plug
attached

New lamp
socket

HOW TO

1 Unplug the lamp and remove the lampshade and bulb. Remove the harp by lifting the sleeves and squeezing the harp sides together slightly and lifting it away (see Fig. A). Remove any felt or cardboard on the bottom to access the cord more easily.

2 With the utility knife, cut the plug off the cord, and secure the wire on the bottom with some electrical tape, so it will not get pulled up through the top of the lamp while you remove the socket.

3 Unscrew the lamp socket from the lamp with a flat-head screwdriver. Look for an area that reads "press" on the lamp socket and press that spot while gently squeezing and twisting the socket out of the cap.

4 Remove the insulating sleeve and outer shell to access the socket itself. The socket will still be attached to the wiring, so loosen the screws where the wires are attached to the socket and unwrap the wires. Now the socket is free to be removed completely (see Fig. B).

continues

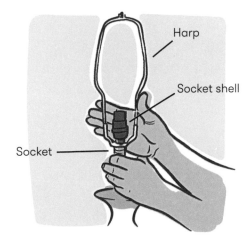

Harp

Socket shell

Socket

Fig. A

Fig. B

continued

Fig. C

Fig. D

5 Pull out the old wiring and feed the new wiring through the lamp. With the new cord fed into the lamp base, leave 6 inches (15cm) of the new cord at the top of the lamp.

6 At the top of the new cord, slice the two halves of the cord apart and pull gently, creating two cords for the first 4 inches (10cm). Using the wire strippers, strip ½ inch (1.2cm) of each half of the cord. Bend the wires of each end of the cord into a hook. Tie an underwriter's knot in the cord (see Fig. C).

7 Identify which of the wires is hot and which is neutral (see page 40). Connect the hot wire to the gold screw on the lamp socket, which is connected to a tab in the center of the socket. Connect the neutral wire to the silver screw, which is connected to the threads.

8 Loop the hook of the wire around the appropriate screw and twist to tighten the screw. Repeat for the neutral wire (see Fig. D).

9 Slide the insulating sleeve and cover back on the socket and push into the socket cap to reinstall. Pull on the cord from the bottom of the lamp so it is taut and reinstall the bottom cover of the lamp.

How to Defrost a Freezer

FROST IN FREEZERS CAN BUILD UP IN A HURRY. Every time the freezer door opens, warm, moist air rushes into the freezer. As the warm air cools, the moisture condenses and lands on racks, walls, and the door. It then turns to frost, and as it continues to build, it takes up valuable space.

YOU WILL NEED

A few large coolers

Several towels

Plastic sheets

Box or pedestal fan

Shallow basin

HOW TO

1 Remove all of the food in the freezer and place it in the coolers. If the freezer is a freezer/refrigerator combo, store the refrigerated food as well.

2 As the freezer defrosts, water will run out onto the floor. If possible, move the freezer to a garage, patio, or deck. Otherwise, lay plastic sheeting on the floor, unplug the freezer, and roll it onto the sheet.

3 Place towels on the racks inside the freezer, especially at the very bottom. These towels will catch most of the water. Be sure to have a few extra towels on hand to replace them as they become saturated.

4 With the doors open, place a box or pedestal fan in front of the freezer. The fan will blow warm air from the house into the freezer, thus hastening the thawing process.

Fig. A

5 If there is a drain hose in the back of the freezer (see Fig. A), place it in a shallow basin to collect the thawed water (see Fig. B).

6 Allow the freezer to thaw completely, drying any water on the floor as it does. Defrosting can take an hour or all day, depending on the amount of frost.

Fig. B

How to Fix a Washer

OF ALL THE APPLIANCES IN THE HOUSE,
the washing machine is the one you least want to break
down. Who wants to make a trek to the laundromat
once a week? Yet, as with most machines that stop
working, there's a good chance that you can get it up
and running again yourself. Here we cover several
issues that could be causing the problem.

YOU WILL NEED

Screwdriver	Owner's	Water pump	Adjustable
Plumber's snake	manual	pliers	wrench or
or wire hanger	Putty knife	Small bucket	socket set

HOW TO

IF THE WASHER ISN'T DRAINING:

1 Check that the drain hose isn't clogged or somehow pinched. If the hose is clogged, use the screwdriver to loosen the clamp and remove it from the back of the washer (see Fig. A).

2 Replace the hose or clear the clog with long, thin material, like a plumber's snake or a straightened wire hanger.

3 If the hose became kinked, reposition it to allow water to flow. If there isn't an issue with the hose, it could be the pump. In which case, refer to the owner's manual to find the pump.

Fig. A

continues

continued

Fig. B

Fig. C

IF THE WASHER WON'T FILL WITH WATER:

1 The water supply hoses might be clogged or bent. Turn off the hot and cold water and use the water pump pliers to remove the hoses from the back of the machine. Be sure to have a bucket on hand.

2 If the small screens inside the hose are clogged with sediment, remove them and clean them out (see Fig. B). Reattach the hoses, open the valves, and try filling the washer again.

3 If the hoses are bent, they might be too long or too short. Use the water pump pliers to remove them from the valves as well, and replace them with the appropriate hose length.

IF THE WASHER DOESN'T SPIN:

1 The rubber coupling between the drum and motor might be worn. You'll have to remove the front cover to access it. Use the putty knife to slide between the top lid and front panel, releasing the clips in either corner (see Fig. C).

Fig. D

2 Use the sockets or an adjustable wrench to loosen the motor mounts to separate it from the drum (see Fig. D). Refer to the owner's manual for a part number to purchase a new coupling.

HANDY HINT

Bent hoses, worn couplings, and other typical failures are often the result of improperly balanced loads. Be sure to balance washer loads as best as possible, and stop the washer immediately if it's out of balance.

How to Fix a Tumble Dryer

IF YOUR DRYER IS SQUEAKING AND BANGING AROUND, it could mean the drive belt is loose, which is an easy fix. It could also be that it's not venting properly. Check the vent to make sure it isn't clogged or that the vent tube isn't kinked.

YOU WILL NEED

Putty knife

Owner's manual

A new drive belt

HOW TO

1 One of the most common failures when it comes to tumble dryers is a slipped or broken drive belt. This belt wraps around the dryer drum, loops under a tensioner pulley, and around a motor. If your drum won't turn on its own or squeaks loudly, this is usually the cause.

2 Unplug the dryer first, and then remove the front panel of the dryer by sliding the putty knife between the lid and the front cover, releasing the clips in the corners.

3 Locate the broken or worn belt and remove it. If the belt is still intact, slip it off the tensioner pulley and remove it (see Fig. A). The tensioner will probably come loose and fall out of its grooves without tension.

Fig. A

Fig. B

4 A local appliance repair shop will be able to match this old belt with a new one, but you might also find the part number in the owner's manual.

5 Slide the new drive belt over the drum and around the motor pulley with the grooves facing downward. Place the tensioner back in its grooves and maintain tension on the spring while slipping the belt underneath it (see Fig. B).

6 Replace the front cover, plug the dryer back in, and test the new belt.

HANDY HINTS

Some dryer drums will remove entirely from the dryer without the front panel in place. They're light but awkward, so enlist the help of a friend if needed.

If your dryer is working but taking longer to dry than usual, the vent could be clogged. Always make sure the vent isn't clogged with lint to ensure hot, moist air can exit the dryer.

How to Unclog a Vacuum Cleaner

VACUUM CLEANERS ARE surprisingly delicate machines, so the first step is to avoid vacuuming anything that can cause a clog in the first place, like large or wet items. For heavy-duty messes, rent a wet/dry vacuum designed for construction and garage use. Before vacuuming, check the canister or bag and empty it to ensure proper suction.

YOU WILL NEED

Flashlight

Broomstick

Wire hanger

HOW TO

1 First, unplug the vacuum. Take apart the vacuum by removing the head and detaching the hose from the body of the vacuum.

2 With the vacuum disassembled, search for the location of the clog. The clog is likely in the head, somewhere along the length of the hose, or at the spot where the hose meets the vacuum. Inspect these areas, using a flashlight if needed, and use your fingers to gently pull out any visible clogs.

3 If the clog is inside the hose and you cannot reach it, use a broomstick to push the clog out. Push gently and slowly to avoid damaging the hose. You can also try running water through a hose to loosen any clogs and debris. Allow to dry thoroughly.

4 If the clog is inside the vacuum itself, try gently reaching in and pulling it out with your fingers. You can bend a wire hanger into a hook and use that to gently pull out a clog if you cannot reach the clog with your fingers (see Fig. A). Work slowly and carefully to avoid puncturing any piece of the vacuum.

5 If you also own, or can borrow, a powerful wet/dry vacuum, you can suction out the clog with the other vacuum. This is an easy way to remove a clog that doesn't risk damaging the vacuum.

6 Once the clog is removed, reassemble the vacuum cleaner and test it. Inspect any clogs to make sure nothing important—like a wedding ring!—was accidentally sucked up and caused the blockage.

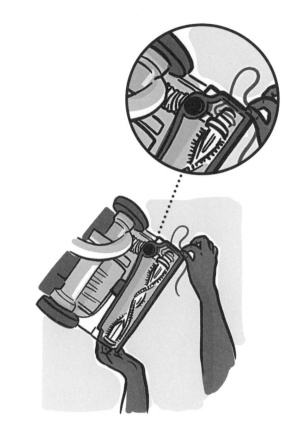

Fig. A

HANDY HINT

If you cannot remove a clog with ease, do not force it. It is better to have it professionally inspected and cleaned than to risk damaging it beyond repair.

How to Paint a Room

How to Repair Blistering Paint

How to Wallpaper a Room

How to Install Wainscotting

How to Lay a Carpet

How to Lay Wooden Flooring

How to Fix Dented Wooden Furniture

How to Regrout Bathroom Tiles

How to Fix a Dresser Drawer

How to Build Shelves

2

Decorating & Upcycling

How to Paint a Room

PAINTING A ROOM is one of the easiest and most cost-effective ways to update a space. Make sure you always use a clean, dry brush. Rinse and lightly dry your roller cover before painting—this will help the roller pick up and release paint. If your flooring is carpet, you may wish to purchase a paint trim guide, which is a long metal tool that you can slide under the trim to protect the carpet as you paint along the baseboard. Use painter's tape to protect baseboards, cabinets, and ceilings from dripping paint. Make sure you remove the tape before the paint has dried, to prevent peeling off fresh paint. Typically, ceilings need a flat paint finish (to hide imperfections), walls have an eggshell finish, and baseboards and trim require a semigloss or gloss finish (for easy cleaning).

YOU WILL NEED

Painter's tape

Drop cloths

24-inch (70cm)
paint trim guide
(optional)

Fast-drying spackle

Putty knife

Safety glasses

80-grit and 120-grit
sandpaper

Dust mask (to use
while sanding)

Primer

Paintbrush

Clean cloths

Paintable caulk

Caulking gun

Caulking
applicator tool
(optional)

Stepladder

Paint stir stick

Paint (see Hints)

Angled paintbrush
2–3 inches (5–8cm)
in width

Paint pad or paint
edger (optional)

Paint tray and liner

Roller handle

Medium ⅜-inch
(7.5cm) roller cover

Extension pole

HOW TO

1 Remove all window coverings, light switch and outlet covers, light fixtures, artwork, and, ideally, furniture. Protect anything you do not wish to paint with painter's tape and lay down drop cloths to protect the floor.

2 Patch holes in the walls (and trim, if needed) with the spackle and putty knife. Once it's dry, use 120-grit sandpaper to sand the spackle so it is smooth and flush with the drywall. Apply a layer of primer with a paintbrush to the spackled areas.

3 If you are painting the trim, lightly sand the entire surface with 120-grit sandpaper to remove any sheen and improve paint adhesion. If the trim is very rough, give it a deeper sanding with 80-grit sandpaper and then use 120-grit to smooth the surface.

4 Wipe off any dust with a damp cloth and apply a thin bead of paintable caulk to any gaps between the wall and top of the trim, smoothing with a caulking applicator tool or a damp cloth and your finger. If the trim was previously painted with an oil-based paint, or is unpainted wood, apply primer.

continues

continued

Fig. A

Fig. B

5 Paint the ceiling first. Dip the first 1 inch (2.5cm) of the angled paintbrush in the paint and then use the side of the paint tray or can to remove excess paint. Push the angle (also called the heel) of the brush against the wall, cutting along the edge. Do one pass with the brush leaving ⅛ inch (0.3cm) from the edge, and then follow up with a second pass to fill in that gap (see Fig. A). Paint a 2-inch (5cm) wide swath of paint along the edges.

6 Apply the rest of the paint with a roller and extension pole. Roll the paint on in small sections. Let dry and apply a second coat if required.

7 For the walls, use the angled brush to apply paint to the corners of the room, as well as above the baseboard, around window and door trim, and at the top of the wall, as in step 5. Push the bristles where you want the line to be and smoothly glide the brush along the heel (see Fig. B).

8 Use a roller to apply paint to the rest of the walls. The roller extension pole allows you to paint from floor to ceiling with one pass. Roll up and down, and back and forth a few times, to overlap and smooth out the paint application. Apply a second coat, if required.

9 Paint any trim last, using an angled brush.

How to Repair Blistering Paint

PAINT TYPICALLY BLISTERS or bubbles for one of two main reasons: moisture or heat (sometimes both). Painting in extreme heat or humidity can cause blistering, as can moisture seeping through a wall or paint applied to a damp surface. However, even something as simple as a dirty surface can cause paint to lift away from soiled areas as it dries. Painting bare drywall without priming first can also cause paint to bubble. Your paint may blister immediately after it dries, but it may also take weeks, months, or years for paint to bubble.

YOU WILL NEED

Safety glasses	Sanding block and 120-grit sandpaper	Paint roller and appropriate roller cover for wall type	Paint stir stick
Dust mask	Spackle (optional)		Paint
Metal paint scraper or putty knife	Primer	Paint tray and liner	

To repair blistering paint, you must first determine the cause. If you are confident that you properly cleaned the wall and primed any bare surfaces, then pick away some of the blistering paint to examine the surface behind it. If only the top layer of paint has blistered, heat is likely the culprit. But if many layers of paint have begun to bubble up, you likely have moisture issues.

Pay attention to the heat and moisture generated in a home from heat-generating appliances, sunlight, and adjacent wet areas, such as bathrooms and laundry rooms. If the issue is moisture or heat from an appliance, the problem in the home must be solved, lest the paint blister once again.

Once any underlying problems are corrected, it is very simple to repair blistering paint. Using a metal paint scraper or putty knife, peel back and scrape off the blistered paint. Sand the affected areas thoroughly, using a sanding block and 120-grit sandpaper. If the blistered area has left a visible dent, fill it with spackle, let dry, and sand smooth. Once the affected areas are smooth and flush with the rest of the wall, apply a quality primer and, once dry, reapply paint. For best results, apply a coat of paint over the entire wall, using a roller and appropriate roller cover. Follow the manufacturer's instructions, typically printed on the can, for the ideal temperature and humidity conditions.

How to Wallpaper a Room

HANGING WALLPAPER TAKES careful planning and a soft touch to get the seams to line up right. It also has the potential of making a big sticky mess. You will need a long work surface to lay the paper on, face down, to apply the glue. In general, be careful not to get any glue on the front face of wallpaper (especially textured papers). Calculate the number of rolls of paper you need by measuring the surface area of the wall to be covered and dividing by 63 (if your wallpaper is 27 inches [68cm] wide) or 56 (if your wallpaper is 20½ inches [52cm] wide).

YOU WILL NEED

Tape measure	Pencil	Masking tape	Paper smoother
Utility knife	4-foot (120cm) level	Paintbrush	
Plumb	Screwdriver	Glue	Sponge

HOW TO

1 Measure the height of the wall to be covered and, using a utility knife, cut strips 2 inches (5cm) longer than needed for extra slack.

2 Go to the middle of your wall and hang the plumb from the ceiling. Draw a line with a pencil and level to where it comes to rest; this is your guide for the first strip of wallpaper (see Fig. A).

3 Remove all switch plates and tape the switches and plugs so they don't get any glue on them.

4 Don't hold back with the glue, particularly along edges and seams. Slap it onto each strip of paper with a paintbrush and "book" the strip by folding it loosely into a concertina (see Fig. B). Glue may squirt out at the sides, so be careful.

continues

Fig. A

Fig. B

continued

5 Take the booked strip to the wall and, starting at the top, unfold it along the plumb line you drew earlier, smoothing it onto the wall as you go. Slide the strip into place, taking care not to stretch the paper.

6 Next, use a smoother to get out any bubbles and get the paper snug into the corner of the wall and the floor. Wipe off any excess glue with a wet sponge and cut off the overlap with a utility knife (see Fig. C).

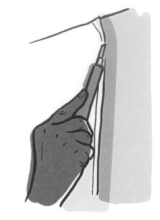

Fig. C

7 Continue this process around the room. Each time you come to a window or switch plate, paste and smooth the strip to the wall before cutting. When you get to a corner, it's okay for the strip to carry over onto the adjoining wall. Just start the next piece right in the corner, overlapping the excess (see Fig. D).

Fig. D

HANDY HINT

Most of the wallpaper choices these
days come prepasted. If using prepasted
wallpaper, loosely roll up a strip, adhesive-
side out, and plunge into lukewarm water,
just until the wallpaper is wet, or according
to manufacturer instructions. Then continue
with the booking process in step 4. These
types of wallpaper may be a little harder
to trim.

How to Install Wainscotting

WAINSCOTTING REFERS TO PANELS applied to the lower section of a wall. Often these panels will be trimmed out with stiles (vertical flat sections) and rails (horizontal flat sections), but there are different styles of wainscotting, including board and batten, raised panel, flat panel, overlay, and beadboard. The type and placement of the panels and molding can dramatically change the look—and the installation method. No matter the method of installation or design, wainscotting is a beautiful way to add architectural charm to a room. Read through this basic installation method to get inspired. Wainscotting is usually installed at approximately a third of the height between the floor and ceiling—about 32 inches (82cm) for a room with 8-foot (2.5m) walls—but you can alter this height to suit your home or style. Adjust this height to avoid awkward spaces between a windowsill and the top of the wainscotting.

YOU WILL NEED

Level	Jigsaw	Air nailer	Paintable caulk
Pencil	Table saw or circular saw	Finishing nails	Wood filler
Stud finder		Nail set	Electrical box extenders (optional)
Painter's tape	Construction adhesive	Miter saw	
Measuring tape	Paneling nails	Caulking gun	Paint and painting supplies (optional)

HOW TO

1 Remove any existing moldings, plus the light switch and outlet covers. You will likely want to remove your baseboards as well, unless they are suitable for working into the new wainscotting design.

2 Using your level and a pencil, mark a level line for the top of the panels across the entire room, measuring to the height of the panels (see Fig. A). Next, find the wall studs with a stud finder and mark those with painter's tape above the level line—this will be useful for the installation process.

Fig. A

continues

continued

Fig. B

Fig. C

3 Measure and cut with a jigaw any holes required for outlets one panel at a time. Working left to right, begin in a corner of the room by installing a panel. Use a table saw or circular saw to cut panels to size, if required.

4 Apply construction adhesive to the back of the panel and set it into place, lining up the top with the level line you marked earlier. Secure the paneling in place on studs with paneling nails and an air nailer (see Fig. B). Repeat for subsequent panels.

5 Complete your wainscotting by installing chair rail or wainscotting cap molding above the panels, then baseboard, with finishing nails (see Fig. C). Or you can cut and install horizontal rails and vertical stiles—the vertical stiles can hide the seams between the panels (see Fig. D).

6 Plan ahead that the seams will align with studs so that the seams and nail holes can be hidden by vertical stiles at the same time. Use a miter saw to cut these trim pieces.

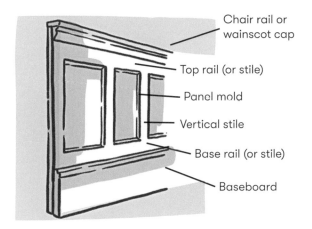

Chair rail or wainscot cap

Top rail (or stile)

Panel mold

Vertical stile

Base rail (or stile)

Baseboard

Fig. D

7 Countersink any holes and, if you plan to paint your new wainscotting, fill any gaps with paintable caulk and fill any visible holes with wood filler. You will likely require electrical box extenders, as the outlets will be newly recessed due to the thickness of the wainscotting.

HANDY HINTS

Always allow wood products to acclimate in the room in which they will be installed for at least 48 hours.

For wood wainscotting, allow 1/16 inch (2mm) between the visible edges as an expansion gap.

For a quicker, DIY-friendly option, skip the paneling and install only the rails and stiles, painting them the same color as the wall beneath to create the illusion of traditional wainscotting.

How to Lay a Carpet

NOTHING FEELS AS PLUSH AND COZY underfoot as wall-to-wall carpeting, but it can be cost-prohibitive. Learn how to lay a carpet to save money. Keep in mind that carpet can be installed in a room in several different ways. This method uses strips of wood, which are filled with upward-pointing tacks. To determine how much carpet to order for any given room, measure the room at its longest and widest points and multiply. That gives you the square footage. To get square yardage, divide that number by nine.

YOU WILL NEED

Knee pads

Vacuum

Nails or masonry
tacks/epoxy adhesive

Carpet tack strips
(also called tackless strips)

Strip cutter or hand saw

Staple gun and staples

Utility knife

Measuring tape

Carpet

Carpet seaming tape

Heat seaming iron

Carpet roller

Knee kicker tool

Carpet trimmer

Carpet stretcher

Carpet chisel

HOW TO

1 Remove old flooring and vacuum the subfloor.
Most carpet manufacturers suggest that you install
baseboards before installing the carpet. Existing
baseboards can stay, as long as there is an appropriate
gap between the subfloor and the bottom of the
baseboard. The required gap will vary, depending on
the thickness of the carpet and padding.

2 Using nails (for wood subfloors) or masonry tacks/
epoxy adhesive (for concrete subfloors), install carpet
tack strips ¼–½ inch (0.6–1.2cm) from the baseboard.
Install them in a straight line, with tacks facing
the wall, along the perimeter of the room (see Fig.
A)—except for thresholds or doorways you will walk
across. Cut tack strips to length using a strip cutter
or hand saw.

continues

Fig. A

continued

3 Install carpet padding next, laying it perpendicular to the direction you will install the carpet and positioned at the edge of the tack strips. Refer to manufacturer's instructions to tape or staple the pieces together. Once the carpet padding has been laid across the entire floor, secure it to the edge of the tack strips using a staple gun. Trim the excess with a utility knife.

4 Cut the carpet to size, leaving 3 inches (7.5cm) extra. Position it in the room, with the nap in the direction you prefer. Where pieces must be seamed together, place seaming tape under the seam. Use a heat seaming iron to melt the glue behind the tape and then use a carpet roller to help secure it.

5 Start at one wall and attach the first edge of carpet to the tack strips. Use a knee kicker tool, which will stretch the carpet over the tack strips and secure it in place (see Fig. B).

6 Trim the excess carpet with a carpet trimmer. Then, using a carpet stretcher, attach the carpet to the tack strips on the opposite side of the room. Repeat for the other sides of the room and finish trimming the carpet. Use a carpet chisel to push the edge of the carpet under the baseboard.

Fig. B

HANDY HINTS

Purchase 10 to 20 percent extra materials (carpet pad, carpet, tack strips). Make sure to purchase the correct kind of tack strips for your carpet. Try to place the carpet seams in inconspicuous areas.

How to Lay Wooden Flooring

HARDWOOD FLOORING ADDS so much value to a home's resale potential. Even if selling isn't on your mind, consider hardwood flooring to add beautiful character and style to any room. Typically, hardwood flooring is installed using a nail-down installation method, while click-lock (or floating) and glue-down (adhesive) are installation methods reserved for engineered wood. Two important tips to remember before beginning the hardwood flooring installation process: install wood flooring perpendicular to floor joists, for strength and stability, and leave an expansion gap—typically around ½ inch (1.2cm), depending on the manufacturer's instructions—around the perimeter of the room. You can buy spacers for this to ensure a perfect gap. Because rooms are typically not perfectly square, do not rely on lining up the flooring boards against a wall. Instead, snap a chalk line where you will begin installation, ½ inch (1.2cm) from the wall.

YOU WILL NEED

Vacuum	Chalk line reel	Drill and drill bits	Flooring nailer
Underlayment or vapor barrier	Hardwood flooring	Finishing nails	Knee pads
Staple gun and staples	Hammer	Nail set	Rubber mallet

HOW TO

1 Remove old flooring and baseboards, and thoroughly vacuum the subfloor, removing any staples or nails. Examine it for damage, or low/high spots, and make repairs.

2 Your subfloor should be level and at least ¾ inch (2cm) thick. Cover the subfloor with the appropriate underlayment or vapor barrier, using a staple gun to secure it to the subfloor.

3 Use the chalk line reel to snap a chalk line ½ inch (1.2cm) from the wall all around the room.

4 To begin installing the wood flooring, choose the longest and straightest planks for the first row. Line them up to your chalk line with the board tongues facing away from the wall (see Fig. A).

Fig. A

continues

continued

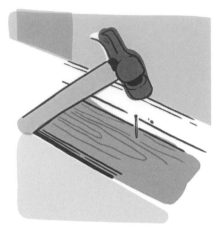

Fig. B

Fig. C

5 Face nail the first row, which means nail through the face of the board (see Fig. B). Drill pilot holes, to avoid cracking or splitting the wood, every 12 inches (30cm) and secure with finishing nails. Countersink the nails using a nail set.

6 Once the first row is installed, you can use a flooring nailer for subsequent rows. Use a rubber mallet to coax any uncooperative boards to fit together to ensure a tight, gap-free installation.

7 Work along the room, installing one row at a time, nailing the planks in place. Wood flooring is sold in random lengths, so consider dry-fitting a few rows at a time to determine an aesthetically pleasing placement of the staggered rows. Only cut boards to length at the ends of the room (see Fig. C).

8 When you get to the last row or two, the flooring nailer may not fit, so you may have to predrill holes and hammer in finishing nails by hand—face nailing, just as you did for the first plank.

Fixing Dented Wooden Furniture

ALTHOUGH SOME WOODS are softer than others, all wooden furniture is vulnerable to dents and dings. Don't despair if your favorite piece of furniture has sustained damage—you can repair the dents yourself.

Some dents can be repaired with only water. For shallow dents in softer woods, try filling the dent with a few drops of water and letting it sit for a day. For larger dents, apply a lightly dampened cloth, folded over a few times, over the dent and press with a warm iron. Both methods will cause the wood to swell, which can raise the dent.

A small dent can also be disguised by touching up the finish. Purchase a felt-tip, touch-up stain pen to match the existing finish and apply to the dent.

For a larger, deeper dent, using a wax filler stick is the easiest option. The wax can be purchased in a color that matches the existing wood finish or natural wood tone. Simply rub the wax stick over the dent, overfilling it slightly. Then smooth the wax so it is flush with the surface, using something with a solid edge, like a plastic putty knife or credit card.

Using stainable wood filler is another option. Lightly sand any rough edges around the dent and then wipe with a tack cloth. Generously apply wood filler with a plastic putty knife. Overfill the dent, because wood filler will shrink as it dries. Allow to set completely and then lightly sand with fine-grit sandpaper, so the filled area is smooth and level with the surface. Then cover the repaired area with stain or paint.

A more advanced method to repair dents is to use a lacquer stick, available in different colors as well as clear. Use a burn-in knife to melt the stick into a creamy texture and apply the melted wax onto the dent. Sand the surface smooth once it dries.

HANDY HINTS

Commercial wood-swelling liquids may also help to raise a dent, if the moist heat doesn't work. When repairing a dent, be careful not to apply heat, filler, or sand beyond the edges of the dent—you do not want to mar the areas where the finish is still perfect.

How to Regrout Bathroom Tiles

THE AVERAGE LIFE SPAN OF GROUT is 10–15 years. Grout is what makes the gaps between tile waterproof, so it's important not to overlook disintegrating grout. If your grout is cracked, has small holes, or is crumbling, then it's time to regrout. Only regrout if the tiles are in good shape and still properly adhered to the wall.

YOU WILL NEED

Rubber gloves

Dust mask

Safety glasses

Utility knife

Grout saw/knife or oscillating tool with grout removal blade or bit

Wet/dry construction vacuum

Grout

Bucket

Rubber grout float

Large sponge

Soft cloth or haze removal

Caulking gun

Caulk

HOW TO

1 Remove any old caulking around the tiles using a utility knife.

2 For best results, remove the old grout so the new grout can properly adhere. You can remove the old grout manually by scraping with a grout saw/knife, but an oscillating tool with a grout removal blade or bit will make this task easier. Be careful not to press the tool against the tile because it may chip. When the old grout has been removed, vacuum the loosened grout debris and dust from the joints.

3 Mix up the grout in a small bucket per the manufacturer's instructions until the grout has the consistency of paste.

4 Using a grout float held at a 45-degree angle, spread the grout onto the tile surface and over the grout joints (see Fig. A). Use firm pressure and apply the grout from alternating directions to ensure that all of the joints are thoroughly filled. As you work, use the grout float to remove excess grout from the tile surface (see Fig. B).

5 When all of the joints are filled, use a sponge that has been very lightly dampened to remove the excess grout from the surface of the tiles and also to smooth the grout lines. Clean the sponge often and wring it thoroughly, working across the surface until the tiles are clean. Once the grout has dried, you will need to clean the haze it leaves behind. You can use a soft cloth to buff the tile surface or use a haze-removing product.

6 Let the grout dry overnight and then replace any caulk that was removed. A week or two after regrouting, apply grout sealer to provide extra stain and water resistance.

Fig. A

Fig. B

HANDY HINT

Tile grout is available as a powder or semiliquid paste and is sanded or unsanded; the latter is best for joints larger than ⅛ inch (3mm).

How to Fix a Dresser Drawer

A DRAWER THAT WON'T CLOSE or otherwise function properly is so frustrating! Learn how to diagnose and fix the most common dresser drawer problems. First, empty the drawer and examine it to assess the problem. Remove the drawer carefully: pull the drawer out as far as it will go and then look underneath, as there may be a small latch or lever to release the drawer. Once it has been removed, pay particular attention to the drawer front (is it still properly attached?), the drawer slides (have they worn out?), and the drawer box (are there bulges along the bottom panel?). Here are some troubleshooting suggestions and quick fixes. Do keep in mind, however, that sometimes wood will swell in humid conditions, so you might find your drawers work better in cooler, drier months and then give you trouble in the summer.

YOU WILL NEED

Screwdriver

Drill and drill bit

Pliers

60-grit and 220-grit
sandpaper

Lubricant (WD-40 or wax)

Nylon drawer
slide tape (optional)

Wood glue

Finishing nails

Hammer

Two-part epoxy (Bondo)

Wood filler

Fig. A

HOW TO

1 Start your troubleshooting by tightening any loose screws with a screwdriver—especially the mounting screws on the drawer slides—and examine the drawer for obstructions. Sometimes a loose nail can prevent a drawer from working properly.

2 If the drawer front has become loose, remove the screws and reinstall it. You will need to drill new holes from inside the drawer's box frame, beside the existing ones. Reinstall the drawer front by screwing it back onto the drawer box.

3 If the drawer slides are causing the problem, examine them for any signs of wear, damage, or, in the case of wood slides, warping or swelling of the wood. Gently straighten any bent metal drawer slides with a pair of pliers. Severely damaged drawer slides may need to be replaced.

4 If you see any shiny areas on the drawer's wood box frame, or on wooden drawer slides, that is a sign that the area is seeing friction, so sanding down the shiny spots with a coarse-grade sandpaper should remedy the problem. Start with 60-grit sandpaper and then switch to 220-grit to sand the wood smooth again (see Fig. A). Sand a little at a time, reinserting the drawer to check for fit to avoid oversanding. If, upon inspection, you see no signs of wear to the slides, then at least give the drawer tracks and slides a thorough clean.

continues

continued

5 Perhaps the issue is simply that the drawer slides require lubrication. For metal drawer slides, apply a lubricant like WD-40 to get the drawer slides operating smoothly again. For wooden drawer slides, you can rub on a bar of soap, paraffin, or wax—even a sheet of wax paper will do. If the lubrication is not enough, you can purchase and apply strips of nylon drawer slide tape.

6 If the drawer box is the issue, it is likely the bottom panel, which bears the weight of a drawer's content and, over time, can sag or warp, preventing a drawer from closing properly. If your drawer panel is sagging, resecure it with wood glue and staples or nails. If the panel is severely damaged or permanently warped, replace it with a new panel.

Fig. B

7 Missing pieces of wood in your drawer boxes can also cause problems, but you can easily patch them. Try a two-part epoxy or wood filler to build back up the missing chunks of wood and repair corners or gauges (see Fig. B). Once dry, sand the area smooth.

How to Build Shelves

SHELVES ARE THE KEY to a tidy, organized home. There are the wall-hung bracketed kind, the freestanding metal kind, or the complex wooden kind made with grooves and joints. One easy way to build a sturdy set of freestanding wooden shelves is to use cleats—small pieces of wood upon which the shelving boards can rest.

YOU WILL NEED

2 boards, 6 feet x 1 x 10 inches (180 x 2.5 x 25cm)

12 cleats, 9 x 1 x 1 inch (22 x 2.5 x 2.5cm)

6 boards, 3 x 1 x 10 inches (7.5 x 2.5 x 25cm)

Sheet of ¼-inch (0.5cm) plywood

6 "lips," 3 x 1 x 2 inches (7.5 x 2.5 x 5cm)

Tape measure and pencil

Electric drill

1½-inch (4cm) flat-head wood screws

Screwdriver

Power saw

HOW TO

1 Lay out the two 6-foot (180cm) boards on the ground. Starting at what will be the bottom of a bookcase, measure up 1 inch (2.5cm) and mark that spot with a pencil.

2 From there, measure every 14 inches (35cm) and make pencil marks at those spots. The bottoms of the shelves will rest at these points.

3 At each pencil mark—and flush with the back of each board—screw in a 1 x 1-inch (2.5 x 2.5cm) cleat, lining up its top with the pencil mark. To make sure the cleat won't split when fastened to the sides, drill three evenly spaced pilot holes into each one, then drive the screw through the cleat face (see Fig. A).

4 Once all the cleats have been attached, hold a 3-foot (1m) "shelf" in place on top of the bottom cleat and drive two screws, equally spaced, through the face of the 6-foot (180cm) board into the end of the shelf.

continues

Fig. A

continued

Fig. B

Fig. C

5 Lay the unit on its side and screw the other end of the shelf to the opposite board (see Fig. B).

6 Leave the unit lying on its side while you secure the top shelf, then the rest of the shelves.

7 Measure and cut the sheet of plywood to fit the back of the shelving unit. Fasten it with screws, spaced every 10 inches (25cm) around its perimeter (see Fig. C).

Fig. D

8 To finish the project, attach a "lip" to the front of the unit, under each shelf. Make sure it is flush with the bottom of the shelf and drive one screw into each end through the outer face of the bookshelf sides (see Fig. D).

How to Remove Stains

Keeping White Clothes White

How to Clean a Bathroom

Keeping a Carpet Clean

How to Sew a Button

How to Patch a Hole in a Pocket

Fixing Glasses

How to Repair a Zipper

How to Reattach a Bag Strap

How to Fix a Shoe Heel

How to Fix a Picture Frame

Refreshing a Cutting Board

How to Sharpen Knives and Scissors

Polishing Silverware

3

Domestic Hacks

How to Remove Clothing Stains

THE QUICKER YOU CAN TREAT a stain, the better. For most stains, it is advisable to pretreat, by blotting with a clean cloth to help draw up the stain, before applying cold water, which can help prevent any stains from setting. Common products around the house can help remove stains, including baking soda, white vinegar, and dish soap. For organic stains, keep an enzymatic cleaner, marketed and labeled as such, on hand. Here are some common stains and tips to remove them.

A clean white cloth

Laundry detergent

Dish soap

White vinegar

Baking soda

Hydrogen peroxide

Enzymatic cleaner

Blotting paper

An iron

Mr. Clean Magic Eraser

Empty spray bottle

HOW TO

COOKING OIL Apply baking soda to a grease stain and rub it in. Let it sit for an hour and then rinse; repeat as needed. If the stain persists, apply a grease-fighting dish detergent over the baking soda and rub gently before rinsing clean. Enzymatic cleaners will work as well.

RED WINE Blot a wine stain with a clean white cloth (see Fig. A) and then apply a mixture of three parts hydrogen peroxide to one part dish soap. Let the mixture sit for 30 minutes to an hour before blotting again with a clean, damp cloth. Reapply until the stain is gone and then launder. Alternatively, apply vinegar and follow up with liquid detergent, before laundering as usual. For items that cannot be laundered, like carpets, blot the fresh stain with a clean white cloth and apply salt or a mixture of one part baking soda to three parts water. Let the baking soda dry, or sit overnight for best results, and then vacuum.

Fig. A

Fig. B

Fig. C

COFFEE Coffee can easily be removed with only cold water. Blot the stain with a clean white cotton cloth (see Fig. A) and then run cold water through the back of the fabric until the stain is removed, and then launder. For a dried or stubborn stain, or a surface that cannot be rinsed, mix white vinegar with powdered laundry detergent to create a paste and let it sit for 10 minutes on the stain before blotting with a damp cloth.

BLOOD Blood stains need to be addressed as quickly as possible. Soak the stain in cold water and use a cloth to apply hydrogen peroxide, rubbing in a circular motion (see Fig. B). Repeat until the stain has disappeared and then launder.

TOMATO SAUCE Apply cold water to the stain and treat with a grease-fighting dish soap. If the stain persists, apply undiluted white vinegar, let sit for 15 minutes, and blot; repeat as needed (see Fig. A). An enzymatic cleaner will work for tomato-based stains as well.

CANDLE WAX Candle wax is best removed once frozen. If the item is small, place it in the freezer. If it is too large, use ice cubes to freeze the wax. Once frozen, the wax can be scraped away (see Fig. C). Sandwich the item between two pieces of blotting paper and press with an iron to remove any residual stains.

GRASS STAINS Soak grass-stained items in cool water and then create a paste with powdered laundry detergent and water to treat the grass stain. Allow the mixture to soak into the stain for an hour and then launder. Alternatively, apply a mix of three parts hydrogen peroxide to one part dish soap. For a stubborn stain, apply an enzymatic cleaner or undiluted vinegar.

SCUFFS Scuffs can easily be removed with a Mr. Clean Magic Eraser but only rub it gently on a surface, as it can also remove the sheen from wall paint.

SOAP SCUM Make your own bathtub or shower cleaner with one part vinegar and one part water, mixed in an empty spray bottle. Add a few drops of grease-fighting dish detergent and spray onto the soap scum. Scrub with a cloth. For stubborn bathtub stains, follow up with an application of baking soda and scrub with a soft cloth.

URINE Press towels into the stain to absorb as much liquid as possible. Mix 1 cup (250ml) vinegar, 1 cup (250ml) water, and 2 tablespoons (25g) baking soda in a spray bottle. Spray the stain and let sit 10 minutes before blotting with a clean white cotton cloth.

HANDY HINTS

If there is still a faint stain after you have treated it, try flushing it out with running water. Water is a solvent and can be used to remove other liquid stains, as well as physically flushing the stain out from the fibers.

If you spill food on your clothes at a restaurant and don't have a white cloth on hand to dab the stain, a piece of white bread will work just as well.

Shampoo is great for removing oil stains. Choose a shampoo formulated for oily hair as the mixture is already designed to break down body oils.

Keeping White Clothes White

FIRST, ONLY WASH WHITES WITH other whites to avoid other fabric dyes depositing color on white garments. You should also avoid washing whites with heavily soiled clothing or in an overstuffed washing machine. In both cases, dirt and grime from other clothes can redeposit onto whites in the wash and make whites look dingy. An overfilled machine doesn't have enough space between items for water to flush away dirt and grime, which means it ends up sticking to other fabric in the machine. Clean your washing machine regularly to ensure that built-up grime and dirt inside the machine isn't redepositing on and discoloring whites.

Adding too much laundry detergent can actually prevent clothes from getting clean because it gets trapped in the fabric and then attracts dirt and helps it stick. Use the appropriate amount for the size of the wash load and shop for a detergent designed for white laundry loads.

Alternatively, add ½ cup (125ml) of Borax or baking soda to your regular detergent to enhance its brightening power.

Use the hottest water your white laundry can withstand, because hot water can help remove body oils and grime.

Line drying whites outside in the sunshine will help naturally brighten white, as the UV rays will help both freshen and whiten laundry.

To help already yellowed or dingy loads of whites, look for a bluing agent to add to the wash load: a product that adds a touch of blue to counteract any yellowing, making old white items appear whiter. For a natural alternative, let whites soak in the washing machine in the hottest water possible, with ½ cup (125ml) of lemon juice added. Soak overnight and then launder as usual.

How to Clean a Bathroom

DEEP CLEANING A BATHROOM is not the most glamorous of cleaning jobs, but it has to be done. The water and steam in your bathroom means it can easily become home to bacteria, fungus, and bad odors. To prevent mildew and other buildup, it's a good idea to deep clean your space at least every one to two weeks.

YOU WILL NEED

Rubber gloves

Bleach-based all-purpose cleaner

Sponge

Nylon-bristled scrubbing brushes

White vinegar

Bucket

Non-abrasive all-purpose detergent

Dry rag

Baking soda

Bleach-based tile cleaner

Old toothbrush or grout brush

HOW TO

TO CLEAN THE TOILET:

1 Put on rubber gloves. Apply the bleach-based all-purpose cleaner to the inside and outside of the toilet bowl.

2 Using a sponge, wipe down all surfaces outside the toilet bowl, including the rim, the seat, and the seat cover. Scrub the inside of the toilet bowl, making sure you get under the rim of the toilet as well as in the plumbing hole.

3 If you have a stubborn ring inside the toilet bowl, turn off the main water supply and flush the toilet. Pour in white vinegar to submerge the ring. Wait a few hours and give the toilet bowl a good, hard scrub. Turn the water back on and flush the toilet.

TO CLEAN THE SINK AND BATH:

1 Fill a bucket with warm water mixed with an all-purpose detergent. Using a nylon-bristled brush, scrub the sink, the bottom and sides of the bath, and any fixtures to remove mineral buildup or bath rings. Rinse everything with fresh water and wipe dry.

2 For soap scum buildup on a sink, sprinkle with baking soda and wait 15 minutes before rinsing. Buff to a sparkling shine with a dry rag.

TO CLEAN THE SHOWER:

1 Spray a good amount of bleach-based tile cleaner onto the grout between the tiles and let it sit for 2 minutes.

2 Put on rubber gloves and, using an old toothbrush or grout brush, scrub the grout until it is clean (see Fig. A). Wipe down grout tiles with a wet sponge and then rinse the tiles and grout with water.

3 To clean shower curtains that have a lot of soap scum buildup, toss them in the washing machine along with a few towels and add ½ cup (125ml) of white vinegar or bleach to the mix. Take the curtain out of the machine before the spin cycle and hang it in the bathroom to dry.

Fig. A

HANDY HINTS

"Hard" water can make bath rings and sink scum worse. If the water where you live has a high concentration of lime or mineral deposits, consider adding water softener to your water supply.

If you don't have tile cleaner handy, make your own mold spray by adding 1 cup (250ml) bleach to 4 cups (1.14l) water.

Keeping a Carpet Clean

CARPET IS GOING TO GET DIRTY—especially the shag variety, which is 10 times harder to keep clean than any other. You should give your rug a deep clean—especially in high-traffic areas—once a year. If that doesn't fit into your schedule, at least get dark-colored carpet to hide the stains, and then call in a professional carpet cleaner to do the dirty work.

Start in one room and move all the furniture in that room out of the way. Then go over the carpet at least twice with a vacuum cleaner to get up loose dirt. Next, use a steam cleaner. These can be expensive to buy, so try renting one. Follow the directions on the steam cleaner and fill the appropriate reservoir with hot water and carpet shampoo.

Starting in a corner, push or pull the steam cleaner's vacuum-like hose over the carpet in long lines with a slow but steady action. Normally, you will press a button to spray hot water and shampoo into the carpet. Once you've done an entire room, do it again but, this time, don't press the shampoo button, so that only hot water comes out and rinses the carpet.

The last step is going over the carpet one more time with the steamer on a different setting, which vacuums up much of the water that went into the carpet. Make sure you don't walk in the room until the carpet is fully dry; this can take up to 12 hours.

HANDY HINT
Never scrub a carpet stain as this can cause the stain to travel deeper into the carpet fibers. Always use a clean white cloth to blot the stain instead.

How to Sew a Button

WHETHER YOU'RE REPLACING a lost button, or updating a garment by replacing all of the buttons with a new style, it's easy to learn how to sew a button. If you're replacing a button, pay attention to the method in which the buttons were sewn on and duplicate that to ensure a seamless look.

YOU WILL NEED

Straight pins

Needle

Thread

Scissors

Replacement button

HOW TO

1 First choose a thread that matches your garment. Thread a needle with double thread, tying in a knot at the end of the thread.

2 Line up the new button where the old button used to be and double check alignment with your garment's buttonhole. Lay a straight pin over the top of the button and make the stitches around the pin, which will keep the tension perfect.

3 Starting from the back of the garment, push the needle through one hole of the button and then thread the entire length of thread through the fabric. Then push the needle back down through the other button hole (see Fig. A). Repeat this process three or four times to secure the button.

4 Remove the straight pin when you have completed these steps. Be careful not to stitch the button on too tight; you want the button to have a bit of play so you can fasten it with ease.

5 On the final stitch, push the needle up through the back of the fabric but not through the buttonhole. Wrap the thread around the button six times, to create a shank, and then push it back down through the fabric (see Fig. B). At the back of the fabric, tie off the thread and trim the excess.

6 For a four-hole button, repeat the process above: push the needle up through the back, through a hole, across to the opposite hole, and back down to the back of the fabric. Sew a few stitches like this before repeating the process on the opposite pair of holes. You will have sewn an "X" and then you can create a shank and secure the thread as above. Some manufacturers sew four-hole buttons with two parallel sets of stitches as opposed to an "X." Duplicate what the manufacturer has done to ensure your new button seamlessly matches the rest.

Fig. A

Fig. B

How to Patch a Hole in a Pocket

THERE ARE A COUPLE OF DIFFERENT METHODS for patching holes in pockets: using a no-sew patch cut from special iron-on mending fabric or stitching the hole closed with thread. The mending patches work well on a surface hole, where perhaps the fabric was punctured or torn, whereas stitching the hole closed works best with a hole along the seam of the fabric.

YOU WILL NEED

Ironing board

Iron-on mending fabric

Scissors

Thin fabric (like a dish towel or scrap of cotton)

Iron

Straight pins

Needle

Thread

HOW TO

PATCHING A HOLE WITH AN IRON:

1 Pull the pocket out of the garment and lay the garment on an ironing board so the pocket can lie as flat as possible.

2 Cut the iron-on mending fabric to size to cover the hole. Lay the patch over the hole and cover it with some thin fabric.

3 Affix the patch with an iron, on medium heat, and gently iron on the mending patch. After 20 seconds, remove the piece of fabric and assess that the patch has been secured by the heat. Repeat if needed, but be careful not to scorch the patch.

STITCHING A HOLE CLOSED:

1 If the hole is along the seam of the pocket, you can also hand-stitch the pocket hole closed. Fold the edge of the pocket over twice and pin in place.

2 Thread a needle with double thread and tie a knot at the bottom. Start on the back of the fabric and bring the needle up through the back to the front.

3 Then in a straight line, approximately ⅛ inch (3mm) away from where the needle came up, push the needle back down to the back of the fabric. This will form a dashed line, called a running stitch (see Fig. A). Work slowly, lest the thread form a knot while you are stitching. Repeat until the end of the area you wish to sew.

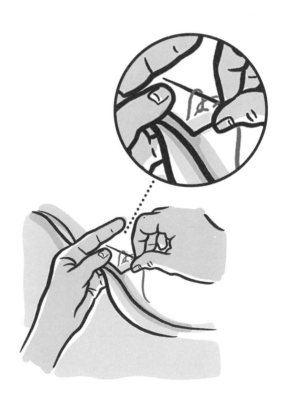

4 To secure the thread, secure the stitches by sliding the needle under the last stitch. Make a loop and then slide the needle through the loop, forming a knot (see Fig. B). Repeat to double knot and cut off the remaining thread.

Fixing Glasses

BECAUSE GLASSES LENSES are often the most expensive part of a pair of glasses, typically costing hundreds of dollars, it might be in your best interest to bring a broken pair of glasses to your optician. Depending on what part of your glasses broke, replacement pieces can be ordered for a fraction of the cost of a full glasses frame. If, however, you're not able to visit the optician, here are some ways to fix your glasses.

If the arms of your glasses have become bent out of shape, you can gently bend them back into shape. For metal arms, simply bend gently by hand or with needle-nose pliers. For plastic arms, heat the arm by running under hot water or holding under a hair dryer for a few seconds. Be careful not to apply heat to the lenses, which can damage special coatings Then gently push the glasses arm back into place. If the frame itself has cracked, add a tiny amount of superglue to the broken area, being careful not to get any glue on the lenses. Remove any excess glue quickly before it dries, with a damp cotton swab. Allow the glasses to dry fully, on a flat surface, before wearing them again.

Repairing or replacing loose hinges and nose pads are the easiest DIY fixes, and you can purchase glasses repairing kits online. These kits typically include the small screwdrivers required to repair a pair of glasses, as well as spare screws and nose pads. Use the included screwdrivers to tighten loose screws or replace nose pads.

HANDY HINT

It's good preventive maintenance to regularly check the screws on older glasses frames to ensure that everything is nice and tight.

How to Repair a Zipper

THERE ARE A FEW DIFFERENT ways that zippers can fail, but before you head to a tailor to pay for a new zipper to be installed, try these tricks for fixing the most common zipper issues. See Fig. A for identifying parts of the zipper. If you don't have zipper lubricant or a graphite pencil, a cotton swab rubbed onto a bar of soap can also help lubricate zipper teeth.

YOU WILL NEED

Pliers

Tweezers or small scissors

Zipper lubricant or graphite pencil

Small brush and dish soap

HOW TO

1 If a zipper splits or separates upon zipping, the problem is likely the zipper slider. If the slider has simply loosened over time, use a pair of pliers to press down on the zipper slider, decreasing the space between the top and bottom of the slider (see Fig. B). Once the space between the top and bottom plate of the zipper slider has been tightened, you should be able to zip the zipper without it splitting.

2 If the zipper slider is damaged beyond repair, simply replacing this one piece of the zipper will fix the problem. Break the old slider off from the zipper with a pair of pliers and slide on the new slider. Push the small metal zipper guard out of the way and slide the slider onto the zipper teeth. If the zipper slider has become attached accidentally, reattach it by feeding the teeth from the bottom end.

3 A splitting zipper can also be caused by zipper teeth that have been pushed out of alignment. Inspect the length of zipper and gently move any displaced zipper teeth back into place using a pair of pliers. Be careful not to snap off any teeth during this process.

4 If the zipper is stuck, there is likely something jammed in the teeth, like a thread or piece of fabric. Use tweezers or small manicure scissors to liberate the obstruction from the teeth of the zipper.

5 If nothing is jammed into the zipper, try lubricating the teeth. You can purchase zipper lubricant, but a graphite pencil works as an easy and relatively mess-free lubricant that everyone has in their home. Simply rub the tip of the pencil against the zipper teeth and the zipper should operate smoothly again.

6 On outdoor garments, corrosion from salt can build up, causing a zipper to stick. Place the garment under a running tap and use a small brush and dish soap to remove any salt and debris. Rinse thoroughly and hang to dry.

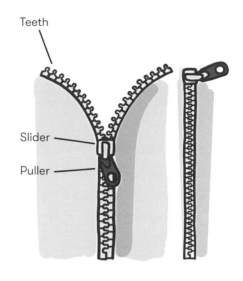

Teeth

Slider

Puller

Fig. A

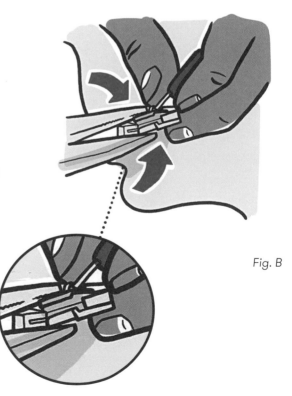

Fig. B

How to Reattach a Bag Strap

BEFORE YOU THROW AWAY AN ENTIRE BAG, know that purse straps can be repaired or replaced. If the strap itself has worn out and cannot be repaired, consider purchasing a new strap to affix to the old bag. If the strap has simply detached or is otherwise salvageable, here's how to fix it.

YOU WILL NEED

Sewing machine

Thread

Needle

Fabric and leather repair quick-dry adhesive

Leather edge coat

Scissors

Small artist's paintbrush

Cotton swab

HOW TO

1 If the strap has torn out of the body of the purse, reinsert the strap into the torn area and use a sewing machine to stitch the bag strap back into place. Sew a rectangle or square for extra strength (see Fig. A), using thread that matches the existing stitching.

2 Alternatively, you can hand-stitch the strap back into place. Thread a needle with a heavy-duty carpet or button thread, and tie a knot at the end. Reinsert the bag strap to where it was torn out of the body of the purse and push the needle up from the inside of the purse to the outside, stitching along where the original stitching was until it feels secure. Then knot the fabric off at the back and trim any extra thread.

3 If the strap has torn away from a leather bag in a way or place that cannot easily be sewn, you can use fabric and leather repair adhesive to reattach the bag strap. Spread a thin layer of adhesive onto the damaged area and press firmly while the adhesive dries.

4 If a leather bag strap has become frayed, or the edges have peeled off, purchase a product called edge coat, which recoats leather edges. Peel away all of the leftover edge coating and trim away any excess with scissors.

5 Take a small artist's paintbrush and apply the edge coat to the purse strap edges, using a cotton swab to remove any excess (see Fig. B). Allow to dry.

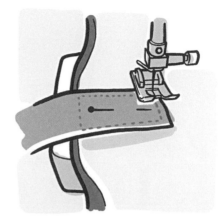

Fig. A

Fig. B

How to Fix a Shoe Heel

DON'T THROW AWAY your favorite pair of shoes simply because the heel has been damaged or lost. Not only can a shoe heel be reattached, you can also purchase new heels if the troublesome heel cannot be used again, whether they are flat, high-heeled, wooden, or leather. Extend the life of your shoes by learning how to fix a shoe heel.

Pliers	Rubber bands	Hammer	Walnut (for wooden heels)
Belt sander (optional)	Utility knife	New shoe heel or shoe caps (for high heels)	
Shoe glue	Cobbler's nails		Liquid leather (for leather heels)

HOW TO

1 If the heel is still partially attached, peel it off the shoe sole using a pair of pliers (see Fig. A). If you have lost one heel, replace both heels on the pair of shoes.

2 Clean the heel and sole of the shoe because any dirt and residue will prevent the glue from adhering properly. If the old glue has left bumps and lumps, use a belt sander to remove the excess glue from the bottom of the shoe. You may sand by hand as well, but a belt sander will offer more precision in keeping the surface flat.

3 Apply a coat of glue designed for shoe repair to both the sole and top of the heel, following the manufacturer's instructions regarding drying time and application. Press the heel and the sole of the shoe together and secure tightly with rubber bands.

4 Weigh down the shoes with something heavy, like a book, if you can, to ensure that the heel and sole are held together tightly while the glue dries. Allow the glue to dry fully.

Fig. A

continues

continued

5 If the new heel is slightly larger than the shoe, you can carefully trim the rubber, so it is flush with the shoe, using a utility knife (see Fig. B).

6 You can also secure a shoe heel in place with cobbler's nails, by hammering the nails into the corners of the heels, with additional nails around the curve of the heel. Space approximately five nails around the heel for strength. Or, if the heel was previously affixed with cobbler's nails, mimic the number and placement of nails for best results.

Fig. B

7 To repair a heel that is simply worn or scuffed, first take stock of the material. For wooden heels, rub an unshelled walnut across the scuff. The oil in the walnut will lift and remove scuff marks. This hack also works for repairing wooden furniture.

8 For a leather shoe heel, apply liquid leather in a color that matches to cover holes and scuffs. The liquid leather can be applied with a cotton swab; to match the texture of the leather, a small textured sheet will be provided. Press that over the repaired area and then let the liquid leather dry for 24 hours.

9 To repair the heel on a pair of high-heeled shoes, look for shoe dowels or shoe caps. These are replacement tips for high heels. Old shoe caps can be removed with a pair of pliers and easily replaced. Instead of using glue, shoe caps can simply be hammered into place.

HANDY HINTS

To protect heels from further damage, purchase an inexpensive set of heel guards to protect from scuffs and scrapes. Always condition leather heels with a special leather conditioner designed for shoes.

How to Fix a Picture Frame

IF YOU RECENTLY KNOCKED over a picture frame while cleaning, or an older frame has just really seen better days, don't despair—here are some easy ways to fix a picture frame and have your favorite piece of art or a treasured photo looking beautiful again. If the glass has broken or cracked, wear protective gloves to prevent cutting yourself. Cracked or broken glass in a picture frame can't be saved, so discard the broken pieces. You can have new glass cut at a glass shop or you can attempt to cut new glass to size yourself.

Work gloves	Utility knife	Clamps or masking tape	Wood filler
Soft towel	120-grit sandpaper	Hammer	Paint or stain
Pliers	Wood or plastic glue	Metal corner braces	
Screwdriver	Damp cloth		

HOW TO

1 First, lay the picture frame facedown on a work surface, like a table or counter. Use a soft towel to protect the surface and also the finish of the frame.

2 To access the glass, remove the picture hanger and also the metal pieces holding the back of the picture frame tight to the frame. Depending on the style, you may need pliers to grip and pull these metal pieces, or a screwdriver to pry them up. Some metal frames will be screwed together in the corners, so unscrew those if applicable.

3 If your frame was professionally made, there may also be a paper backing. Gently cut that away with a utility knife. Then disassemble the frame, separating the backing, picture, and glass.

4 If the frame has come apart in a corner, lightly sand the areas where the frame meets with 120-grit sandpaper and apply glue to the joint. For wood frames, use wood glue, but for plastic frames, purchase a glue suitable for the material. Remove any excess glue with a damp cloth immediately after applying. Assemble the frame and clamp the corner (you can use masking tape for this, if you do not own any small clamps), then allow the glue to dry overnight.

continues

continued

5 Sometimes a corner will simply come loose over time. If it is held together with screws, tighten them, and if held together by small finishing nails, hammer the nails gently to tighten the frame corner. To reinforce the corners of a picture frame, screw on four flat metal corner braces, one onto each corner (see Fig. A). This can help tighten a loose corner joint and is an easy fix for most frame styles.

Fig. A

6 If a wooden frame has been gouged or damaged on the surface, use a paintable/stainable wood filler to fill the damaged area. Overfill the area (as wood filler shrinks), and then sand smooth once dry with 120-grit sandpaper (see Fig B). Once the filler has dried overnight, stain or paint the repaired area—paint will ensure a seamless and near-invisible repair.

7 Once repaired, reassemble the frame by placing the glass first, then the photo or art, then the backing. Use a hammer or pliers to reinsert the metal pieces keeping everything together. Reattach the hanging hardware and enjoy your repaired picture frame.

Fig. B

HANDY HINTS

Glue is best applied to unpainted and unstained materials.

There are spray paints designed for wood, plastic, and metal, which create a nearly factory-like finish when applied in thin, even coats.

Refreshing a Cutting Board

WOODEN CUTTING BOARDS are workhorses in the kitchen and can eventually look very worn. Luckily, a wooden cutting board can easily be refreshed and restored to like-new condition with little effort.

To remove cuts and dents from the wood, sand the surface, along the grain, with 80-grit sandpaper wrapped around a sanding block (optional). When you have removed deep cuts and dents, wipe with a tack cloth or soft cotton cloth to remove dust and then switch to a finer 120-grit sandpaper. When you are satisfied with the surface of your cutting board, wipe with a damp cloth to raise the grain, and then finish up the sanding process using 220-grit sandpaper. Wipe once more with a damp cloth to remove any dust and let dry.

You may notice that your cutting board is much lighter in color after the sanding process. Oiling the wood will restore the richer wood tone while protecting and conditioning the wood. You can use what is in your cupboard for conditioning wood, like olive or coconut oil, or use food-grade wood oils designed for wooden cutting boards and spoons. Use a soft, clean cloth to apply the oil all over the surface and let it soak into the wood for a few hours. Remove the excess by buffing with a clean, dry cloth until you can no longer feel the oil.

HANDY HINTS

Never put a wooden cutting board in the dishwasher. Hand-wash promptly after use and immediately dry with a dish towel. To really deep clean, wipe the surface with vinegar or sprinkle the surface with salt and scrub with a lemon cut in half. Reapply wood oil once a month to keep your cutting board looking like new.

How to Sharpen Knives and Scissors

OVER TIME, KNIVES AND SCISSORS can become dull. It's inevitable: regular use will dull blades, and dull blades can be frustrating to work with—and become unsafe. Note: the long, tubular honing steel that may have been sold with your knife set doesn't actually sharpen your knives! What it does is help hone the blade, straightening it back out a bit.

YOU WILL NEED

Knife sharpener

Whetstone (or sharpening stone)

HOW TO

1 Place the knife sharpener on a stable surface and put the knife in the divot. Pull the knife toward you in one swift movement, using firm and even pressure, doing a few passes on the coarse side and then moving to the fine side. Be sure to hold the knife straight—do not let it tip side to side (see Fig. A).

2 A more advanced method is to use a whetstone. Completely soak the whetstone and then hold the knife against the coarse side of the whetstone at a 20-degree angle. Press the knife down, applying light pressure, and drag it across the whetstone, making sure the heel and tip of the knife all make contact with the whetstone, while maintaining the same angle the entire time (see Fig. B).

3 Repeat for both sides of the knife, dragging the knife along the whetstone approximately 10 times for each side. Repeat with the fine side. For a really damaged knife, you may need many more passes across the whetstone. Make sure the whetstone remains wet the entire time.

4 To sharpen scissors, use the same whetstone you used for sharpening knives, remembering to keep it wet at all times. Lay the inside surface of one blade against the stone and sharpen the same way you sharpened the knife blades: apply light, even pressure and drag the blade across the stone. Repeat 10 times and then sharpen the other blade. Then repeat both blades on the fine side.

Fig. A

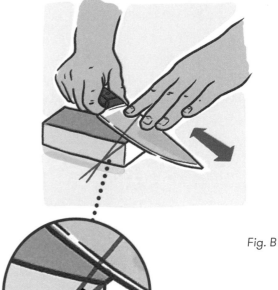

Fig. B

approximately 20° angle

HANDY HINTS

Do get a knife sharpener that has both a coarse and a fine side.

Test your knife's sharpness by slicing into a tomato to assess how cleanly it slices through. Keep sharpening if your knife doesn't pass the test. For scissors, test by cutting a sheet of paper.

Polishing Silverware

USING THE GOOD SILVERWARE always adds a festive touch to any occasion—but not if the silverware is tarnished beyond recognition. Luckily, there are a few easy ways to polish silverware, from using commercial silverware polishes to using kitchen staples.

Fine silverware, made of real silver, should always be hand-washed and regularly polished to avoid excessive tarnish. The more heavily a piece is tarnished, the more difficult it is to restore to its former luster, so regular cleaning and maintenance is key. After washing, hand-dry immediately to avoid water spots.

If fine silverware has tarnished, restore it to its former glory with silver polish. Follow manufacturer's instructions and then immediately rinse with hot water and dry quickly and thoroughly to avoid water spots. Silver polish is available in many forms: sprays, wipes, foams, and more. You can also purchase soft cloths that will help remove tarnish by simply rubbing the silverware with it.

For a more natural solution, try soaking silverware in a mixture of ½ cup (125ml) of vinegar and 2 tablespoons (25g) of baking soda. Soak for two hours and then inspect—if the silverware is still not as shiny as you'd like, soak for another hour and then rinse with hot water and dry immediately. Remove stubborn tarnished spots by creating a paste with water and baking soda, scrubbing the silverware gently with the paste and a soft cloth.

If you need a more thorough polishing, or have ornate silverware that is difficult to clean, boil water and line a heat-resistant dish with aluminum foil. Add ½ cup (125ml) of vinegar and 1 cup (250ml) boiling water to the foil-lined dish. Lay the silverware in the water and vinegar solution and let soak for 30 minutes. Buff any remaining tarnish off with a soft cloth. Keep your silverware in a felt-lined box to keep it tarnish-free.

How to Paint the Outside of a House

How to Lay a Concrete Tile Patio

How to Install a Dead Bolt

How to Service Gutters

How to Replace an Asphalt Roof Shingle

How to Repair Roof Flashing

How to Fix a Sagging Gate

How to Repoint Brick Walls

4

Exterior Fixes

How to Paint the Outside of a House

PAINTING THE OUTSIDE of your house is not difficult and will make a huge difference to the way your house looks. Most of the job is prep work—sanding, scraping, washing, and filling nail holes. The painting itself takes up hardly any time at all.

YOU WILL NEED

Dust sheets

Bristle brush

Bleach

Water

Scraper

Various-grit sandpaper

Dry cotton rags

Hammer

Nail punch

Masonry filler

Putty knife

Oil-based primer

Ladder

Oil-based or cement paint

1½- and 2½-inch (4 and 6cm) paintbrushes

Small paint bucket with liner

Bucket ladder hook to secure paint on the upper rungs

Stirring stick

Masking tape

HOW TO

1 Cover shrubbery and flower beds with dust sheets, and trim shrubs or trees so they won't brush against the house after the paint goes on. Remove anything fixed to the outside of your house that may get in the way of painting.

2 Clean the exterior of the house, including under windowsills. If mildew is discoloring any unpainted woodwork, mix a solution of one part bleach to three parts water and scrub the area with a brush. Rinse with regular water.

3 Locate any painted woodwork that's blistered, peeling, or cracking. Scrape or sand the area, then wipe it with a damp rag.

4 Go around the house and set nails below the surface of any wood with a nail punch. After setting a nail, fill it with masonry filler (see Fig. A). Once this has dried, sand it with a fine-grit sandpaper.

5 Prime all bare wood on the exterior of the house and let the primer dry overnight. Start painting from the top of the house down: set a ladder to reach the eaves of the roof.

6 Paint the woodwork, again from the roof down. Always paint windows from the inside out: first the sash (which holds the glass), then the sides, top, and bottom of the window, then the outer molding.

Fig. A

HANDY HINT

Wet paint left to dry in direct sun will blister, so paint the west-facing walls in the morning and east-facing walls in the afternoon.

How to Lay a Concrete Tile Patio

LAYING YOUR OWN PATIO is a simple job that will keep your guests comfortable (and off the lawn that you spent all summer mowing). Concrete tiles come in many colors and shapes, from bricklike rectangles to large squares to interlocking "bow ties," and can be installed without any messy mortar.

YOU WILL NEED

Concrete tiles of your choice

Shovel

Hand or power tamper

Crushed granite

Sand

4-foot (120cm) level

Hammer and chisel

Push broom

HOW TO

1 Stake out the patio area and use a shovel to dig out the soil to a depth of about 6 inches (15cm). Tamp it down firmly with a hand or power tamper (see Fig. A).

2 Fill in 3 inches' (7.5cm) worth of crushed granite. To prevent spillages or rain from pooling on or under the finished patio, gently slope the patio by ⅛–¼ inch (3–6mm) per foot. Tamp it down firmly as you go.

3 Fill in 2 inches (5cm) of sand on top of the granite, and screed the sand into a smooth base.

4 After you have waited four weeks, lay the concrete tiles, leaving ¾ inch (2cm) between each one (see Fig. B). Use a hammer and chisel to cut any tiles to fit once all of the whole ones have been laid.

5 Pour more sand on top of the tiles and sweep it into the gaps with a push broom.

Fig. A

Fig. B

HANDY HINTS

An existing concrete patio or walkway can be tiled as long as any cracks in it are level. If one side of the crack is higher than the other, do not tile over it.

Concrete shrinks and gains strength for weeks after it is poured. Wait at least four weeks before tiling over a new concrete slab.

How to Install a Dead Bolt

A DEAD BOLT CAN ONLY BE OPENED BY a key or thumb turn (unlike a spring latch, which can be forced open with a knife or credit card). This makes them a good choice for preventing forced entry. Here's how to install a dead bolt if you don't already have one. To maximize your home security, make sure you buy a lock with the longest bolt possible.

Tape measure	Dead bolt kit with	Drill with ⅞-inch	Hammer
Pencil	bolt, template, face	(22mm) spade bit	Black shoe polish
Square	plate, striker plate,	and a 2½-inch (6cm)	
Boring jig	and lock	hole saw	
	Chisel		

HOW TO

1 Measure up 6 inches (15cm) above the doorknob or above the latch bolt on your door and make a pencil mark. Use a square to draw a straight line through this mark. This line will run through the middle of the circle needed to hold the dead bolt.

2 Place your template on the door. It should fit on the edge of the door, folding over from front to back. Line up the mark from step 1 with the corresponding mark on the template and use a pencil to transfer the reference points from the template to the door. These will show you where each hole needs to be drilled, including the one on the edge of the door where the bolt itself will go (see Fig. A).

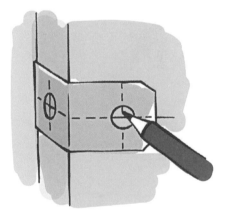

Fig. A

continues

continued

3 Use a drill outfitted with a 2½-inch (6cm) hole saw and bore out the main hole in the face of the door. Before the saw passes all the way through the door, stop drilling and finish the hole by sawing from the other side.

4 Change the hole saw for the ⅞-inch (22mm) spade bit and drill into the edge of the door to create a hole for the bolt to go through.

5 Put the bolt in the hole and position the face plate over it, in order to trace its outline on the edge of the door. Then chisel out the edge of the door so that the face plate will be flush with the wood once it is screwed in place (see Fig. B).

6 Fit the dead bolt together and secure it in place with screws. Screw on the face plate.

7 Dab the end of the bolt with black shoe polish, close the door, and open the bolt into the door frame, leaving a black mark. This will determine where to drill for the dead bolt in the door frame.

Fig. B

8 Repeat step 5, this time with the strike plate, tracing its outline and chiseling the door frame out so that the strike plate will be flush with the wood. Screw the strike plate into place.

How to Service Gutters

LEAVES, TWIGS, ACORNS, dead insects, and other detritus will fill and clog gutters by the end of fall, so giving them a thorough clean both before and after the season is a good idea. (If you live under a bunch of trees that shower their leaves more than most, you might want to check the gutters a few times during the fall as well.)

YOU WILL NEED

Garden gloves

Ladder

Bucket or garbage bag

Garden hose

Drainage rod

Screwdriver

Silicone sealant

Wire brush

Putty knife

Waterproof cement

Scrap of aluminum

HOW TO

1 Put on some gardening gloves and climb a ladder to access the gutters. Scoop out leaves and other debris with your hands and place into a bucket or garbage bag.

2 Once you've cleared away the debris, use a garden hose to run fresh water along the gutter (and out the downpipe) as a cleanser.

3 If the downpipe is clogged, use a spray attachment on the end of the hose to send a jet of water down the opening. If that doesn't work, use a drainage rod to push the clog out.

4 Walk around the perimeter of your house and check for loose screws where sections of gutter meet each other, especially at downpipes. Also, check for loose gutter brackets. Tighten either as you go with a screwdriver and fill gaps in the metal with silicone sealant.

5 If the gutter has a hole in it, you can patch it. When it is completely dry, use a wire brush to scuff up the area around the tear or hole inside the gutter. Then use a putty knife and apply waterproof cement to the area around the hole.

6 Bend a piece of aluminum flashing to fit the round contour of the gutter and push it into the waterproof cement around the hole (see Fig. A). Apply more waterproof cement around the edges of the patch.

Fig. A

HANDY HINTS

If any part of the gutter is rusted, torn, and full of holes, don't try to patch it. Just replace the entire section.

When patching a hole inside a gutter, don't put so much waterproof cement on it that you create a dam that prevents water from flowing to the downpipe.

How to Replace an Asphalt Roof Shingle

ASPHALT SHINGLES HAVE BEEN AROUND for over a hundred years, and they're by far the most popular roofing material in modern times. They're relatively inexpensive and tough, and manufacturers have figured out how to make them last for decades—50 years, in some cases! But, in the course of a shingled roof's life, damage can happen. Particularly violent windstorms, fallen branches, or even thrown objects such as baseballs can peel back a shingle. With the shingle pulled back, rain, snow, bugs, and other undesirables can damage the structure underneath and cost big bucks. So, instead of letting Mother Nature have her way with your bare roof, you need to replace the asphalt shingle. As long as you're comfortable with heights and your roof isn't too steep, you can tackle the job.

YOU WILL NEED

Fall protection
harness and rope

Ladder

Flat pry bar

Hammer

Matching shingle

Utility knife

Roofing nails

Roofing cement
or caulk

Caulking gun

HOW TO

1 Donning a fall protection harness anchored properly, climb the ladder onto your roof. Carefully work your way over to the damaged shingle.

2 The nails that are holding your damaged shingle in place are hiding underneath the shingle above it. Carefully slide the pry bar under the shingle on top of the damaged shingle, separating the sticky tar and revealing the nails underneath (see Fig. A). Be careful not to damage any shingles that are still in good shape. Hot shingles can become very soft and pliable, so be careful when separating them. If you're too hasty, the pry bar can rip through good shingles you didn't intend on replacing.

3 With the top layer lifted, use the pry bar and hammer to remove the nails holding the damaged shingle in place. Generally speaking, there will be four to six nails driven along the strip of sticky tar.

continues

Fig. A

4 The damaged shingles will most likely still be sticking to the shingles below them, as well. Use the flat bar to carefully separate the damaged shingle from the row below it. At this point, the damaged shingle should be loose and can be easily removed.

5 Lay the new shingle on the roof in the old shingle's space. If the new shingle is too long, carefully trim it with a utility knife. If the new shingle is too short, cut two to fill the gap.

6 With the new shingle in place, nail it into the roof with four to six nails. Be sure to nail through the strip of tar to create as watertight a seal as possible (see Fig. B).

7 With the roofing cement or caulk in the caulking gun, squeeze a small dab of adhesive under each corner of the new shingle's tabs, as well as the tabs of the shingle above it. The tar will become sticky and grab the shingles within a few sunny days, but the roofing cement or caulk will keep them in place until then.

Fig. B

HANDY HINT

You might have to loosen the row of shingles above the damaged shingle, as well as the next row above that. Architectural shingles usually require two rows of nails, the higher of which will be underneath the second row above the damaged shingle.

How to Repair Roof Flashing

WHILE YOU ARE UP on the roof replacing a tile, check the flashing—the strips of metal found around chimneys and vent pipes and along roof valleys and eaves. These strips are fastened with nails and waterproof cement in places where water has the best chance of leaking into a house. They can get old and come loose, or simply start to corrode.

YOU WILL NEED

Hammer

Waterproof cement

Silicone sealant

Strips of aluminum roof flashing

Wire brush

Putty knife

HOW TO

1 Check flashing at any seams and near its edges. Look for nails that have wiggled loose, crumbling or missing roof cement, or any spots that have been bent away from the roof surface.

2 Rehammer loose nails, then cover the nail heads with waterproof cement.

3 If you see crumbling roof cement or if the metal is bent away from the roof, add more cement or silicone sealant to fill the gap and bend the metal back into place if possible.

4 If flashing is corroded or has started to form holes, you can patch sections of it with strips of similar metal. First, scuff the surface of the old flashing with a wire brush.

5 Use a putty knife to apply a coat of waterproof cement to the scuffed surface of the old flashing and push the metal patch into the cement and over the corrosion or hole (see Fig. A).

6 Cover the patch with some more waterproof cement.

Fig. A

HANDY HINT

If you've installed new flashing, keep in mind that it can look conspicuously shiny. You may want to paint it and touch up existing flashing to blend in with the roof. Use a zinc-based primer and then spray on two or more light coats of rust-inhibiting metal paint.

How to Fix a Sagging Gate

AH, THE QUAINT COTTAGE-FEEL of a garden gate. They allow passage for friends, pets, lawn equipment, wheelbarrows, and many other things into the backyard. But as time goes on and the natural elements take their course, the wood wears and the gate begins to sag. The gate might strike the ground or not latch, and there's nothing "cottagey" about that. As long as the post the gate hangs from is in good shape, fixing a sagging gate is rather simple. All it takes is a bit of hardware and some careful adjustment, and even the oldest of gates will start to swing properly again.

Material to prop or shim the gate to the correct position

Speed square or framing square

Anti-sag gate kit

Screwdriver

Power drill

Linesman pliers

HOW TO

1 Start by closing the gate and propping it to the correct position. Use rocks, bricks, or other materials to rest the gate upon to hold it in place. Checking the gate by eye is fine, but a speed square or a framing square tucked under the top rail and placed against the post provides a better gauge.

2 The gate kit should contain two brackets. Attach the top bracket on the corner of the rail on the hinge side of the gate. Attach the bottom bracket on the corner of the latch side of the gate (see Fig. A).

3 Adjust the turnbuckle so it's holding on by just a few threads on either end. Hook the turnbuckle into the top bracket (see Fig. B).

continues

Fig. A

Fig. B

continued

4 Thread about 6 inches (15cm) of the steel cable from the kit through the bottom bracket and double it over (see Fig. C). Use a screwdriver to secure it in place with the included cable clamp. On the other end, thread the steel cable through the bottom loop of the turnbuckle so the wire is tight between the two points. Clamp it in place with the other cable clamp, but don't cut the wire yet.

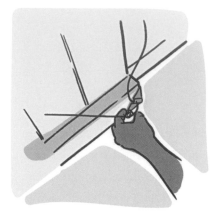

Fig. C

5 Adjust the tension on the line by tightening the turnbuckle (see Fig. D). As soon as your tightening lifts the gate off the material propping up the gate, remove the material. Use the speed or framing square to check the gate and adjust accordingly.

6 Once you're satisfied with the alignment of the gate, use the linesman pliers to snip the ends off of the steel cable. It's best to leave an inch or two on either end in case adjustments are necessary in the future.

Fig. D

How to Repoint Brick Walls

BRICKS ARE TOUGH but they can get dirty and the mortar that holds them together can crumble. Like anything else outside your house, brick walls need to be cleaned and the old mortar has to be replaced—a process called repointing.

YOU WILL NEED

Hammer

Chisel

Brick mortar

Small bucket

Brick trowel

Pointing trowel

Large, old paintbrush

Hydrochloric acid

Water

Long-handled, stiff-bristled brush

HOW TO

1 Rake out old and crumbling mortar with a hammer and chisel. Mix up the mortar in a bucket. Scoop mortar onto a brick trowel, spread in place, and use a pointing trowel to push the mortar into the gaps between the bricks (see Fig. A).

2 When enough mortar has been pushed in, dip an old paintbrush in water and rub it gently on the brick and the mortar joint to compact the mortar even more (see Fig. B).

3 Let the mortar dry for half an hour, then use the tuck pointer to slide off any excess, making the mortar flush with the brick.

4 Allow the mortar to dry overnight, then mix a cleaning solution of one part hydrochloric acid to 10 parts water in a bucket.

5 Dip a long-handled, stiff-bristled brush in the solution and scrub the brick and joint. This should clean the brick of any film or grime that's left over from the repointing.

Fig. A

HANDY HINT

Before you begin repointing, give your brick wall a good soaking with a hose and leave it overnight. This hydrates your bricks and old mortar, meaning that they won't suck the water out of the new mortar you are about to add.

Fig. B

5

Backyard & Shed Hacks

How to Build a BBQ Pit

WHY SPEND THOUSANDS OF DOLLARS on a gas grill when you can build your own barbecue pit for way less? And if you love to barbecue, what's better than having your own custom-made pit in your backyard? Make sure you pick the best spot—you don't want it too far from the house that you have to carry the food and utensils a long way, but you want it far enough away that it won't blow smoke into your (or your neighbor's) house.

YOU WILL NEED

Two metal BBQ grills

Iron tray to hold the
coals and ashes

SX-grade paver bricks or
SW-grade face bricks

Pointed trowel

Mortar

Chalk line

Hand level

Rebar

HOW TO

1 First, buy your BBQ grills and coal tray. Whatever size you choose will determine the size of the pit. Then calculate the number of bricks you'll need. This pit is 13 layers high at the sides with three more layers at the back for a wind block. One side and the back are three layers deep. The other side is nine layers deep.

2 If you already have a patio, find an area where a BBQ pit is at a safe distance from the house. If you don't have a patio, you'll have to build one. (A spot on your lawn is not level or sturdy enough to support the weight of a BBQ pit.)

3 Measure out the perimeter of the pit and snap chalk lines to use as guides. Do a test run with the first layer of bricks by laying them down on the slab, leaving ½ inch (1.2cm) between each brick to compensate for the mortar.

4 Remove the bricks and, with your trowel, put down a layer of mortar. Set the first bricks inside the chalk lines, remembering to add mortar to their sides as you go.

continues

continued

5 Stack each layer of bricks on top of the one before it, mortaring and cleaning the brick faces as you go (see Fig. A). Use a hand level to check for level and plumb as you build.

6 When you get to the eighth layer, embed lengths of rebar in the mortar so that about 4 inches (10cm) of it sticks out into the center of the pit. Do the same for the ninth and twelfth layers (see Fig. B). These will be the supports for your two grills and the coal tray.

Fig. A

Fig. B

Choosing a Lawn Mower

WHEN THE TIME COMES TO BUY a lawn mower, it's a good idea to visit a local showroom and try them out. There are several different types of lawn mowers. The most popular are:

HAND-POWERED MOWER Manual mowers are essentially push mowers. They may have an engine, but it only operates the blades and doesn't provide momentum. Muscle power, as opposed to electric, battery, or gas power, is what gets this mower moving. These mowers are the quietest, most environmentally friendly, and the most inexpensive. They also require a good amount of strength and energy so are best suited to small lawns.

ELECTRIC MOWER An electric mower uses a standard engine with an extension cord. When using these mowers, be careful that hauling the cord around your garden doesn't ruin a freshly mowed lawn.

GAS-POWERED MOWER Heavier than the previous mowers, a gas-powered mower has an engine that runs on gas and therefore isn't restricted by a cord and is great for mowing large areas. Easy to steer, gas-powered mowers are strong enough to cut dense or tall grass and maneuver fairly well around obstacles. They do need to be regularly serviced.

BATTERY-POWERED MOWER Battery-powered mowers are not tied down to a power source, making them well suited to yards of any size. Keep in mind that many of these mowers will run for about an hour before they need to be recharged. Batteries will also need to be replaced every few years.

Whatever kind of mower you opt for, the best way to mow your lawn is to start at the perimeter. Work back and forth across the lawn in even strips, overlapping slightly so you don't miss any patches.

How to Fix a Lawn Mower

KEEPING A FINELY MANICURED LAWN takes dedication and a trusty lawn mower. But as with anything mechanical, lawn mowers are prone to their share of issues. Luckily, the solutions tend to be pretty straightforward and within the capabilities of most DIYers. Here's how to fix a gas-powered lawn mower.

YOU WILL NEED

Spark plug (optional)

Hot water

Fresh fuel

Socket wrench

Metal file

IF YOUR LAWN MOWER WON'T START:

1 Gas-powered mowers need three things to run: air, fuel, and ignition. If one of those is missing or working improperly, the mower won't start. Start by checking the spark plug. If the plug is covered in gummy fuel, fouled with soot, or covered in corrosion, replace it.

2 Next, check the fuel system. Most mowers have in-line filters or filters on the end of the fuel pickup line inside the tank. Make sure this filter isn't clogged or filled with gummy fuel.

3 Finally, check the air filter. These are often clogged with grass, dust, pollen, seeds, and other small particles from mowing the lawn. You can normally wash air filters with hot water.

IF YOUR LAWN MOWER STARTS BUT ISN'T CUTTING EFFICIENTLY:

1 Ensure that there is enough fuel in the tank and that it's less than a month or two old. The fuel filter might be too clogged to provide enough fuel. This filter is usually in-line with the fuel line running to the engine or on the end of the pickup tube in the tank (see Fig. A).

2 If your lawn mower appears to be running well but isn't cutting efficiently, it's probably a case of dull blades. You can buy replacements, but they're easy to sharpen on your own. Remove the spark plug wire so your lawn mower won't start.

3 Use a socket to unbolt the blade (or blades) underneath the mower. Using a metal file, restore the blade's edge by passing the file in one direction, matching the angle of the existing bevels (see Fig. B).

4 If your mower is running well but feels like it's vibrating, the blade is probably out of balance. Remove the blade and hang it from its mounting hole on a nail driven partially into a wall. The side of the blade that drops is too heavy, so remove more material with the file.

Fig. A

Fig. B

Fixing a Dead Grass Patch

LUSH, THICK GREEN GRASS makes quite the first impression. Nothing ruins that ideal picture like a dry, brown, dead patch of grass. Grab your work gloves, some tools, and a bit of grass seed so you can get to the bottom of it.

Use a rake to remove the mat of dead grass on the surface of the soil. This material is known as "thatch," and it prevents air, light, and water from penetrating the soil and nourishing the grass. Rake the surface in different directions to remove as much thatch as possible.

Improve airflow and water penetration by aerating the soil in the patchy area with a lawn aerator. Holding the handle in both hands, step on the aerator to drive it into the soil. Continue aerating every 6 inches (15cm). Any soil plugs from the aeration process can be left to decompose, or you can rake them out and remove them.

Next, spread grass seed over the freshly aerated soil. Use the rake to lightly scratch some of the seed into the dirt. Spread a few handfuls of hay over the seed. The hay will retain moisture and also prevent birds from snacking on the grass seed.

Water the seed with the hose and nozzle or set up a sprinkler. New grass seed needs watering two to three times each day, for around 5 minutes at a time. Once the grass seed germinates and sprouts begin to show, move to watering for a longer duration (30–45 minutes) two or three times a week.

Controlling Garden Pests

GARDEN PESTS gnaw leaves, damage fruit, and trample plants. But you can't watch every leaf and bud every minute of the day. Here's how to tackle some common garden pests, plus some more general advice on preventing them.

One of the best ways to offset the damage from pests is to provide your plants with high-quality soil. By using natural fertilizers, compost, and other soil-enriching additions, you'll be providing the plants with the nutrients they need to grow strong and resist the effects of pests.

Insects like ladybugs, parasitic wasps, lacewigs, hoverflies, and spiders are worth keeping around as they eat other pests. You can order these bugs online or attract them with insectary (pollen and nectar-producing) plants. For the bold, hunting and transplanting praying mantis nests into your garden can be a tremendous help with pests.

Many insects and small animals will avoid the scent of strong-scented plants and herbs. While you can plant calendula, cilantro, and garlic annually, you can also opt for perennials like anise hyssop, chives, and thyme, which may repel pests.

Another way to create plant-based pest control is to interplant your crops. Pests love large swaths of the same plant, so mixing up rows of vegetables with pest-repelling plants and flowers can confuse them, making it harder to establish themselves in the garden.

Pests are inevitable, but it's best to avoid them at all costs until your plants are strong enough to handle their presence. Covering your plants with row covers or hoop houses will keep them safe until they're established. If you prefer to keep them covered for the long haul, make sure to lift the covers for a few hours each day to allow pollinators in.

How to Fix a Cracked Flowerpot

FLOWERPOTS CAN BE fragile, and small bumps and drops can turn into cracks and splits. But all is not lost; many broken pots still have years ahead of them. All it takes is some fast-setting glue, some time, and a bit of patience, and a cracked pot can be back on its feet—or saucer, more likely.

YOU WILL NEED

Clear, fast-setting glue

Rubber gloves

Respirator mask
(optional)

Masking tape

Medium-grit
sandpaper

HOW TO

1 Start by choosing the correct glue. Look for glue that sets quickly, dries clear, and is suitable for use both indoors and out. Most importantly, ensure that it works with ceramics.

2 Clean any dirt from the cracks or along the edge of the broken pieces. The dirt will prevent the glue from penetrating the crack and sealing it off.

3 If there are a few broken pieces, test-fit them all to ensure you know how they fit. They can feel like a puzzle, but it's best to figure it out before breaking out the glue.

4 Put on some rubber gloves. If the glue is noxious, be sure to work outside or in a ventilated area. A respirator mask never hurts, either. Starting at the lowest broken piece, glue along the crack in the pot as well as the matching edge of the missing piece (see Fig. A). Insert the piece, being sure to seat it into its place. For extra support, stretch masking tape around the outside of the pot to hold the piece in place as it dries.

5 Once the glue dries, use additional glue to seal the cracks from inside the pot. Drag the tip of the glue along each crack and push the glue in with a gloved finger (see Fig. B). Continue along all of the remaining cracks.

6 Once everything is dry, remove the tape and sand the edges and cracks with medium-grit sandpaper.

Fig. A

Fig. B

HANDY HINT

There is a good chance you'll still be able to see the cracks after the repair. Consider painting the pot—this will hide the cracks and breathe new life into an old flowerpot.

Removing Leaf Stains from a Deck

MOST FOLKS EITHER love fall for its beauty or loathe it for signaling the end of summer and the onset of winter. One thing they can agree on is that leaf staining on a deck's surface isn't one of the season's better characteristics. Let's talk about removing them.

Those leaf stains can be stubborn, but they aren't unconquerable. Mixing 1 cup (250ml) of dish soap into a bucket of warm water is often all it takes. Just soak the stained area in the solution and allow it to work its way into the wood's pores for 10 minutes. Then, armed with a stiff scrub brush, give that stain a good scrubbing to lift it.

Be sure to rinse the area thoroughly afterward. The sun can cause your cleaning solution to evaporate before it reaches its full potential, so wait for a relatively cloudy day if your deck is in direct sunlight.

If those stains need a bit more power, you can take a heavier-handed approach. Mix 1 cup (250ml) of ammonia into a bucket of water and pour it over the stained area. To improve the staying power, lay an old towel over the stained area and saturate it with the ammonia solution. After 10–15 minutes, remove the towel and use a stiff scrub brush to loosen up the stains. Rinse the area with a hose afterward.

You may have to break out the pressure washer, but don't go full bore at first. Instead, use the widest, gentlest nozzle you have to soak the deck with a deck-cleaning solution. Allow it to soak in for a few minutes to break up the stain's bond. With a more aggressive nozzle (no more than 15 degrees), give the area a thorough washing. Be sure to hold the tip of the pressure washer at least 8 inches (20cm) from the deck's surface to prevent damage to the boards.

Storing/Protecting Garden Furniture

AFTER SPENDING MANY SUMMER nights lounging on your patio or backyard furniture, it's never fun to start thinking about storing it when the temperature starts to get cooler. But taking the extra time to properly store your patio items can help them last for many years to come.

The most important thing to remember before you put your outdoor furniture away for the winter is to clean it to prevent mold or mildew (it doesn't hurt to do this once a season while you're still enjoying the furniture too).

To clean wooden furniture, use a mixture of 1 cup (250ml) ammonia, ½ cup (125ml) vinegar, ¼ cup (50g) baking soda, and 1 gallon (4.5l) of water and gently scrub. Let the wood air-dry before storing. For extra credit, apply a protective sealant to protect the furniture from moisture damage year-round.

Plastic furniture doesn't have issues with moisture; however, colder temperatures can make the plastic brittle enough to crack, so you should bring in these pieces before it gets too cold. Use a mixture of dish soap and water to clean the furniture first, rinse the pieces, and let them air-dry.

If you have cushions with removable covers, read the manufacturer's recommendations for cleaning. If possible, take the covers off and put them in the washing machine on a gentle cycle. For cushions that should not be machine washed, use a dry cloth and sturdy brush to apply a mild detergent. Let the covers/cushions air-dry before storing.

After the deep clean, either store the furniture in a shed or garage, put a tarp over it, or shrink-wrap it. Even if you have custom-made outdoor covers for your sofa, you should place the pieces in storage, secure a tarp over them, or shrink-wrap them.

Winterizing Plants

NO ONE WANTS TO SPEND HUNDREDS of dollars each spring buying new flowers and plants for our gardens, but somehow we can't get around it. This guide to protecting your annuals or tender perennials from the cold will break that cycle.

The easiest and most effective way to protect outdoor shrubs is to spread a new layer (about 3 inches) of mulch around the base of your plants, leaving 1 ½ inches free from the stem for air circulation. For perennial and flower beds, lay a layer of 6–8 inches of wood chips on top. For roses, mound 12–18 inches of soil around the base. And for young tree trunks, wrap them in burlap.

Any potted plants should be brought inside your house, garage, or basement, depending on space. This should be done before the year's first frost. You should also check for any pests or disease before bringing your plants inside—use a plant spray of your choice.

You can also dig up plants with bulbs, tubers, and corms. Remove all the dirt and allow them to dry, then store them in a cool, dry, and dark place during the winter and replant them again in the spring.

HANDY HINT
Know your plants and how much sunlight and humidity they might need to survive inside. But keep in mind that even professional nurseries and garden centers have a hard time overwintering their plants—if you fail the first time you try it, don't give up!

Putting Up Backyard Lighting

PUTTING UP OUTDOOR LIGHTING can improve your home's social atmosphere. But where should you put up your lights? And what type of lights should you use? The answer depends on the situation and goal.

Lights used to highlight plants, water features, fences, walkways, and even the house can boost the appeal of the home. You can find most of these lights in solar-powered options, which makes customizing your outdoor lighting a breeze.

One of the best ways to light up an outdoor sitting area is by hanging outdoor-rated string lights. Each individual bulb gives off a soft light, but with enough of them spread around the patio, deck, or firepit, they'll ensure the party can continue when the sun goes down.

Tree limbs make great anchor points for string lights, especially if they're central to the seating area. Simply drape string lights from a big tree to the roof of your house, or keep the string lights to the tree branches themselves.

For wider expanses, consider driving wooden posts into the ground and using metal cable routed through eyelets as support wire. Simply zip-tie the string lights to the support wire and run the lights from post to post. You can always camouflage the wooden pole with a potted plant. The heavy base of the planter will keep the post stable, while the flowers and greenery will add some beauty to this setup.

How to Repair a Bicycle Tire

RIDING A BICYCLE can be a blast, but we often take those rubbery, shock-absorbing cushions we call tires for granted. We crash them into potholes, roll over sharp objects, tear them up with heavy braking, and deform the sidewalls with hard cornering. Any one of these situations could result in a flat tire, and that's no fun for anyone. Does a flat mean that the tire is garbage? It depends. Aside from some custom setups for expensive bikes, the tire doesn't actually hold air. There is a balloon-like tube inside the tire, and it's this tube that goes flat. Luckily, most holes in this tube are patchable. But if the crash or debris was especially rough, or the tire is old and dry-rotted, replacement might be a good idea. With this guide, you'll know how to patch or change a tire, regardless of the circumstances.

YOU WILL NEED

Adjustable wrench

Bicycle pump

Marker or chalk

Bike tire repair kit

2 tire levers,
wooden spoons,
or similar

New bicycle tire

New inner tube

HOW TO

1 To fix a tube or a tire, the wheel needs to come off the bike. If the bike doesn't have quick-release hubs, use an adjustable wrench to remove the entire wheel.

2 The tire needs to be completely flat. Remove the cap on the valve and press the metal tip inside to release the air (see Fig. A).

3 It's best to remove the tube before the tire to prevent damaging it. Start by pulling the tire to one side of the rim to reveal the tube. Pull the tube out from under the tire and off of the rim. Lift the tire valve out of the wheel and remove the entire tube (see Fig. B).

4 Find the hole in the tube. If it's not evident, use the bicycle pump to fill the tube with a bit of air (10 PSI is plenty). Listen for the leak. If it's still difficult to find, fill a sink with water and hold the tube underwater until the bubbles appear. Note the location with your finger, remove the tube, and dry the area off without losing the leak's location. Take a marker or piece of chalk and mark a circle around the leak.

Fig. A

Fig. B

continues

continued

Fig. C

Fig. D

5 Most bicycle tire repair kits come with a bit of sandpaper. Use it to scuff the area around the leak lightly. The slight scratches in the rubber will give the adhesive in the next step something to hold on to.

6 Place a small amount of the adhesive from the kit around the hole. After waiting about 5 minutes for the adhesive to become tacky, place a rubber patch from the kit over the hole and hold it in place for several minutes.

7 If the tire is damaged, remove it from the wheel by hooking the tire levers (or wooden spoons) under the tire and prying it off the rim. This often requires two levers and a bit of patience. Slide one lip of the new tire onto the rim (see Fig. C).

8 Inflate the new patched tube just enough that it holds a round shape, and then place the tire valve through the hole in the rim. Tuck the rest of the tube under the tire all the way around the wheel (see Fig. D).

9 Being careful not to pinch the tube, stretch the other lip of the tire up and over the wheel, using the tire levers to carefully maneuver it into place. Ensuring the tire is sitting evenly around the rim, inflate the tire completely and check for leaks.

How to Fix a Bicycle Chain

HITTING THE TRAILS, track, open road, or a simple parking lot on two manually powered wheels can be a lot of fun. But whether you're grinding up some single track or pushing for top speed, a bike chain is under a lot of tension and torque. With a bit of neglectful maintenance or misalignment, the chain can pop loose, twist, kink, or react in several other ways. Some damage is repairable, while other chain snafus require a new chain. Either way, you don't need to take the bike to a shop. Save money and do it yourself. Here's how.

| Spray lubricant | Bike chain tool | Replacement chain | Master link |

HOW TO

1 Kinks are often the result of corrosion, so a bit of spray lubricant could be all it takes. Squirt the kinked link with lubricant, allowing it to soak in for roughly 20 minutes.

2 To stretch the link, position the link on the top half of the chain by turning the pedals backward. With the rear brake engaged, put a bit of forward pressure on a pedal to straighten out the chain.

3 Chains that snap can be fixed with a master link. Use the chain tool positioned over the rivet (see Fig. A) to remove the broken link. Repeat this on the other end of the chain to remove the other broken section.

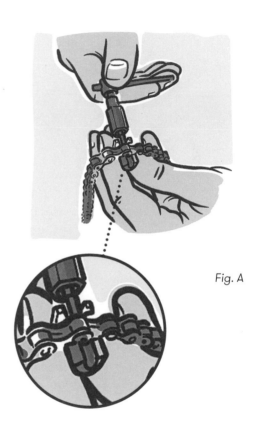

Fig. A

continues

continued

Fig. B

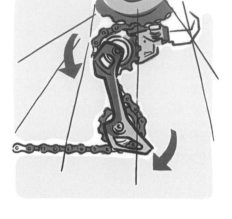

Fig. C

4 Position one half of the master link in each end of the chain, overlapping each other (see Fig. B).

5 Seat the link by positioning it on top of the chain, holding the rear brake, and putting forward pressure on the pedal until you feel a slight click.

6 Twists usually involve several inches of chain, and they need replacing. Use the chain tool to break the chain and remove it from the bike.

7 Shift the bike so that the derailleur (the spring-loaded tensioner that aligns the chain) is set for the lowest (largest) gears. Route the new chain through the derailleur and over both the low gears (see Fig. C).

Fig. D

8 Push the derailleur forward so it's slightly less than fully extended. Note where both ends of the chain meet and use the chain tool to remove the excess length (see Fig. D). Use the supplied master link to fasten the chain.

HANDY HINTS

As a general rule, it's a good idea to replace your bicycle chain every 2,000 miles.

Cleaning your chain regularly with an old rag and applying bicycle lube will keep it running smoothly and prevent damage.

Chain replacing is easiest with the bike held in an upright position or on a bike stand.

Save excess chain if it's still in good shape. You can reuse it to replace sections of twisted chain in the future.

How to Fix a Skateboard Wheel

BELIEVE IT OR NOT, homemade skateboards have been around for more than a hundred years. The sport's pioneers started by removing the wheels from their roller skates and attaching them to a plank, and the fun ensued. It wasn't until the late 1950s that commercial skateboards became available, and with their invention, specialized wheels and hardware were soon to follow. Whether you have a longboard or shortboard, skateboard wheels are durable, as they have to take the wear that speed, tricks, slides, and jumps cause. But, as cool as those maneuvers might look, they do beat up the wheels and the bearings they house. The good news is that skateboard wheels are serviceable, so a broken wheel doesn't have to take the board out of commission.

Socket set

Ratchet wrench

Replacement wheel

Replacement bearings (if they're worn)

Hair dryer

HOW TO

1 Start by removing the nut that holds the wheel in place on the axle or "truck"— the official name. Choose a socket that fits snugly on the nut to prevent stripping it.

2 Using the socket and ratchet wrench, turn the nut counterclockwise until it's free. If there is a washer on the axle, remove it as well. Save these, as the replacement parts won't come with extra hardware.

3 The wheel should be loose, but if you're reusing the bearings, you need to use the axle to remove them. Lift the wheel so the tip of the axle clears just the outer bearing (see Fig. A).

Fig. A

continues

continued

Fig. B

Fig. C

4 Rock the wheel back and forth, using the axle to pry the inner bearing from the wheel. Flip the wheel over and repeat the process until both bearings (and the spacer between, if any) are out of the wheel (see Fig. B).

5 Inspect the bearings to ensure they're in good condition. If not, consider replacing them. Place the inner bearing on the axle. Place the dust shield (usually a markedly darker ring on one side of the bearing) toward the middle of the skateboard. Next, place the spacer (if there is one) on the axle, followed by the wheel (see Fig. C).

6 With the skateboard on its top and placed on your lap, seat the bearing by pulling the wheel toward you. It helps to heat the wheel slightly with a hair dryer (especially with shortboard wheels), though it's not always necessary. Just be careful not to melt the wheel with too much heat.

7 Remove the wheel and place the other bearing on the axle with the dust shield facing the middle of the skateboard (see Fig. D). Repeat the seating process by pulling the wheel toward yourself.

Fig. D

8 The bearings should be in the wheel, but they won't be fully seated. Orient the wheel on the axle so that the desired side of the wheel is facing outward. Place the washer back on the axle, followed by the nut.

9 Use the socket and ratchet wrench to tighten the nut. As the nut tightens, it will squeeze the bearings into place, fully seating them. Spin the wheel to ensure it spins freely. If not, loosen the nut slightly until the wheel spins freely.

HANDY HINTS

Some bearings have dust shields on both sides. The dust shields will be black or dark gray in comparison to the rest of the bearing. If that's the case, you can place them in the wheel with either side facing out.

Replacement wheels usually come in sets of four, while replacement bearings come in sets of eight. You don't need to replace everything at once, but if the tools are already out, it might make sense to service all four corners of the skateboard at once.

Where to Buy Your Tools

BASIC HAND TOOLS are available in many stores, but you should generally avoid buying them at the grocery store or pharmacy; purchasing tools at your local hardware store or home center is a better alternative. Large chain home centers supply a good selection of the more common tools, though they may not have some of the more unusual items. And the likelihood of obtaining knowledgeable assistance can be haphazard. Hardware stores may have fewer large items, but they're often better sources for hand tools and fasteners and expert advice.

When it comes to expensive hand tools and larger shop tools, you'll want to visit larger hardware stores, tool dealers, and woodworking stores for the best selection.

Buying tools online—especially power tools—is now a mainstream option. It's still a good idea to research the products and check them out in person, and even if you buy from a traditional vendor, it doesn't hurt to compare online pricing.

Be wary of unusually low prices. Sometimes sellers will advertise the basic tool for a reduced price, but charge for accessories usually included in the list price. In other instances, the retailer may be offering reconditioned tools, which are those that were originally faulty and returned to the manufacturer for repair. This isn't always a bad thing, because it means the company has thoroughly checked and tested the tool prior to resale, but you should be aware of this prior to your purchase.

You can also buy used tools. This is a good way to obtain a particular tool for a reduced price, or a higher quality of tool than you would normally afford. Try garage sales, flea markets, and used-tool dealers. If you decide on this option, familiarize yourself with the tool as new beforehand. It's easier to notice any problems or defects you may encounter, and you'll learn the difference between a quality tool and a piece of trash. Generally, look them over and ensure they are in good condition. Check for bent parts or cracked castings. Clean them off a bit to make sure all the pieces are present, otherwise it may be impossible to find replacement parts. You can ignore a little surface rust, but if anything looks especially rusty or pitted then it's worth bypassing.

When purchasing more substantial tools like a table saw or a drill press, investigate the tool's history. You may be buying a saw from a hobbyist woodworker who has been puttering around with it in the basement, or from a contractor who has bounced it on and off his truck six days a week. Ideally, you'd like to find lightly used and well-cared-for tools.

WHEN BUYING USED TOOLS

Ask why the owner is selling it. The answers may give you a clue to any potential problems with the machine.

Verify the availability of replacement parts before you buy, and think about how much you need to invest before it is operational.

Obtain from the owner whatever accessories, safety equipment, manuals, and documentation originally came with the tool. They will make the operation safer and repairs and maintenance easier.

About the Authors

TOM SCALISI is a writer and editor specializing in home improvement, construction, and men's interest. Having worked as a mechanic and a contractor, his writing is rooted in his experience and passion for DIY. He has written for a wide variety of publications, including *This Old House* magazine, *Bob Vila, Levelset,* and more. He lives in Hudson Valley, New York, with his wife and children.

TANYA WATSON runs the popular blog Dans Le Lakehouse, where she documents the DIY renovations and interior design of her Canadian home situated on the edge of Lake Superior. Tanya is passionate about repurposing thrifted items to give them a new life, and has attracted over 100,000 monthly blog viewers with her budget-friendly projects and ideas. Tanya has collaborated with *Elle Decor, Buzzfeed, Country Living, Better Homes & Gardens*, and many more.

SAM MARTIN is the former editor of *This Old House* magazine, and the author of several books, including the popular *How to Mow the Lawn* and *Manspace: A Primal Guide to Marking Your Territory*, the latter of which he has adapted into a TED Talk. His writing has appeared in *Dwell, Metropolis,* and *Natural Home*. He lives in Texas with his two sons.

Glossary

Caulk: a material used to seal joints or seams against leakage in various structures and piping.

C-clamp: a C-shaped device for securing workpieces to a bench or template during fitting, joining, gluing, or assembly.

Chisel: a cutting tool used to shape, carve, and sharpen materials like wood, cement, bricks, stone, and metal.

Circular saw: a power tool that cuts materials using a round blade, often used by cabinetmakers and carpenters.

Drywall: also known as plasterboard, a building material made of two sheets of thick paper with plaster set between them, used for inside walls and ceilings.

Drywall saw: a long, narrow saw used for cutting small, often awkward features in various building materials.

Epoxy: a type of polymer used as glues and adhesives to make laminated wood.

Grout saw: a manual tool used to remove old and discolored grout (a composite material generally consisting of water, cement, and sand) from joints.

Hacksaw: a hand-powered, small-toothed saw used for cutting hard materials such as metal or plastic.

Hole saw: a saw blade of annular (ring) shape, allowing the user to bore out a circular hole in the workpiece without having to cut up the core material.

Jigsaw: a power tool which uses a reciprocating blade to cut irregular shapes and curves, such as stenciled designs, in wood or metal.

Linesman pliers: recognized by a stub nose, flat gripping surfaces, large cutting edges, and their angular edges on the outside of the jaw. Mostly used for electric alterations such as to straighten, cut, grip, twist, push, and pull wire.

Miter saw: a powered saw with the blade mounted on a swing arm that pivots left or right to produce a variety of angled cuts.

Needle-nose pliers: both cutting and holding pliers with long, slender jaws used for small or thin objects.

Pilot hole: a small hole drilled into a piece of construction material, often used to guide the insertion of a larger drill or hole-making tool.

Primer: a coating applied to a surface to prepare it for painting.

Pry bar: a small, flattish iron bar used in the same way as a crowbar.

Putty knife: a broad, flat metal blade or spatula used to mix or apply putty.

Rebar: a steel bar or mesh of steel wires used in reinforced concrete.

Spacer: a device used to create or maintain a set distance between two objects, such as between steel reinforcement and formwork when concrete is poured.

Spackle: a paste or compound made of gypsum powder and binders and used to patch small holes.

Spark plug: a device in an engine that produces an electrical spark that lights the fuel and makes the engine start.

Speed square: a multipurpose triangular carpenters' tool used for the measurement of distance and angles; its functions include many of those of a combination square, try square, and framing square.

Table saw: a mechanical saw powered by an electric motor and secured to the underside of a table so the cutting edge protrudes above the surface and can usually be adjusted to change the cutting depth and angle.

Wire strippers: a small handheld tool that is used to remove the insulation from electric wires.

Index

Thunder Bay Press
An imprint of Printers Row Publishing Group
9717 Pacific Heights Blvd, San Diego, CA 92121
www.thunderbaybooks.com • mail@thunderbaybooks.com

Copyright © 2022 Elwin Street Limited
Conceived and produced by
Elwin Street Productions
10 Elwin Street
London E2 7BU
United Kingdom

All rights reserved. No part of this publication may be reproduced, distributed, or transmitted in
any form or by any means, including photocopying, recording, or other electronic or mechanical
methods, without the prior written permission of the publisher, except in the case of brief
quotations embodied in critical reviews and certain other noncommercial uses permitted by
copyright law.

Printers Row Publishing Group is a division of Readerlink Distribution Services, LLC.
Thunder Bay Press is a registered trademark of Readerlink Distribution Services, LLC.

Correspondence regarding the content of this book should be sent to Thunder Bay Press, Editorial
Department, at the above address. Author or rights inquiries should be addressed to Elwin Street
Productions at the below address.

Thunder Bay Press
Publisher: Peter Norton • Associate Publisher: Ana Parker
Editor: Dan Mansfield
Acquisitions Editor: Kathryn Chipinka Dalby

Elwin Street Limited
Editor: Anja Schmidt
Designer: Matt Ryan
Illustrator: Olivia Whitworth
Image credits: Alamy: pp 33, 101, 157; Shutterstock: pp 7, 9, 17, 24, 38, 43, 59, 65, 73, 77, 79, 85,
89, 97, 107, 115, 119, 121, 125, 135, 141, 147, 155, 161, 163, 167, 171, 175, 180.

Library of Congress Control Number: 2021952802

ISBN: 978-1-64517-946-7

Printed in the United Arab Emirates

26 25 24 23 22   1 2 3 4 5